A pictorial history of **SURFING**

A pictorial history of SURFING

by
FRANK MARGAN
and
BEN R. FINNEY

PAUL HAMLYN
London   Sydney   New York   Toronto

EDITOR'S NOTE

The photographs, old prints and wood engravings in this book have come from a multitude of international sources and I wish to sincerely thank all those who contributed them. In particular I am most grateful for the material supplied by Agnes Conrad, the Public Archives, Honolulu, Hawaii; Judith Reed, Bernice P. Bishop Museum, Hawaii; Le Roy Grannis, California; Tom Blake, Florida; Nadine Kahanamoku, Hawaii; 'Snow' McAlister, Rex Phillipps, Ken Watson, Pat Henderson and Jack Eden, Sydney; and Barry Brown of the National Council, Surf Life Saving Association of Australia. I would also like to acknowledge the personal assistance of Patricia Curran, New York; Sue Mayhew, London; and Wendy Lehane, Doug Holleley, Ruth Dunbar and Ian Head, Sydney.

Barbara Leach

Published by Paul Hamlyn Pty Ltd, 176 South Creek Road, Dee Why West, New South Wales 2099

First Published 1970

Copyright Paul Hamlyn Pty Ltd 1970

Printed in Melbourne by Wilke and Company Limited, 37-49 Browns Road, Clayton, Victoria.

National Library of Australia registry number ISBN 0 600 36955 2

Registered in Australia for transmission by post as a book.

CONTENTS

ACKNOWLEDGEMENTS

Following is a list of acknowledgements for pictorial material used in this book. While every effort has been made to obtain permission to use the illustrations, in some cases it has proved impossible and we therefore wish to convey our thanks to any unnamed or untraceable persons or organizations whose material is contained herein.

Alby Falzom
Atlas to Cook's Voyages 1784
Ted Ashby
Australian Associated Press
Australian News and Information Bureau
Doc Ball
Bernice P. Bishop Museum, Hawaii
Tom Blake
Bondi Surf Life Saving Club
Brisbane Courier-Mail
Camera Features
Beverley Clifford
Ben Cropp
Daily Mirror Newspaper
Daily Telegraph Newspaper
Leo H. & Suzanne P. Duyckers
Jack Eden
Mary Evans Picture Library, London
Florida Cypress Gardens
Freelance Photographers Guild
Le Roy Grannis
Hawaiian Visitors Bureau
Pat Henderson
Heroes of the Surf by Reg. S. Harris
David Hill
Honolulu Star Bulletin
Dr Don James
Nadine Kahanamoku

Keogh Surfboards, Sydney
Jean H. Labaysse
Life in the Sandwich Islands 1851
   by Henry Cheever
'Snow' McAlister
Manly Art Gallery
Manly Daily Newspaper
Manly Surf Life Saving Club
Mansell Collection, London
Mid Pacific Magazine
David Milnes
David Mist
Mitchell Library, Sydney
National Fitness Council of N.S.W.
Our Hawaii by Charmian Kittridge
Marshall Perhan
Petersen Publishing Company, California
Rex Phillipps
Peter Pike
Polynesian Researches 1831 by William Ellis
Public Archives, Hawaii
Qantas Airways Limited
Peter Rae
Randwick Historical Society
Jim Russell
Smiths Weekly August 10, 1935
Rodney Sumpter
Sunday Times February 22, 1920
Surfabout Magazine
Surf and Suburban News 1917-18
Surfing, The Sport of Hawaiian Kings
   by Ben R. Finney & J. D. Houston
Barrie Sutherland
Sydney Morning Herald Newspaper
Town & Country Journal February 18, 1914
Tyrrells Bookshop, Sydney
United Press International
Jozef Vissel
Ken Watson
Bob Weeks
West Australian Newspaper

Surfing's Hawaiian Past

Riding a surfboard across the breaking face of an ocean wave has recently become an international sport enjoyed by hundreds of thousands of surfers along continental and island shores around the world. Surfing is not, however, a new sport, nor is it a Western creation. Two centuries ago it was primarily a Polynesian sport, and among the Polynesians, the surfers of old Hawaii were the most expert. Today's world wide surfing movement stems from the ancient Hawaiian sport, which in turn developed from a more rudimentary wave-riding tradition brought to Hawaii by the first Polynesian settlers of a thousand or more years ago.

All surfers, ancient and modern, have had at least one thing in common: the waves they ride. Whether or not a wave is rideable depends on the right combination of ocean swells and shoreline configuration. Strong ocean swells, generated by storms far out at sea, that strike a gradually sloping beach, an underwater reef or a jutting headland usually produce the best surfing waves—those that rise steeply, but break with a regular curl and leave an open shoulder in front of the moving break so a surfer can ride free of the tumbling white water. Three main ways have been developed to surf such waves: body-surfing, canoe surfing and surfboarding. Surfboarding was in ancient times and is again today the most popular,

The biggest wave ever ridden? According to the story, in 1868, Holaua Kauai was washed out to sea on a tidal wave. Grabbing a passing plank, he rode the next wave, a 50 footer, right back to shore. From a painting by C. P. Cathcart in the Bishop Museum, Honolulu.

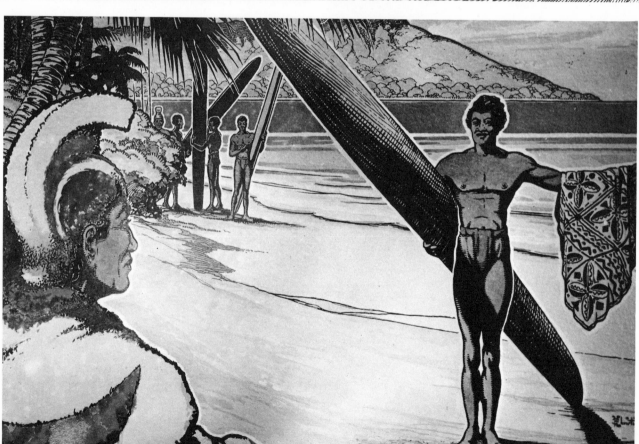

Great watermen were the early Hawaiians.
In canoes such as these shown above
they travelled all over the Pacific.
From *Atlas to Cook's Voyages 1784.*

The early Hawaiians surfed all around the rocky shores of their islands. The picture shown, above left, by a 19th century artist, shows the typical old style Hawaiian surfing in contrast to modern Waikiki with its gentle waves and soft sandy shore.

A young Hawaiian Prince salutes his ruler before surfing.

spectacular and exciting of the three. Kneeling or lying prone on a surfboard, the surfer uses his hands and arms to paddle out to where the surf peaks. Just before it breaks, he paddles before a moving wave until he has enough speed and the wave's slope is steep enough for him to slide free. The surfer then stands and manoeuvres the board with his body weight and footwork to stay at the edge of the breaking wave, darting in and out of its curling edge as he surfs toward shore.

The first step in developing this form of surfing may have been the discovery by a swimmer that a wooden plank held before a breaking wave was a handy device for speedily returning to shore. Such a discovery could have led to the simplest form of surfing—belly-board surfing—using a short board held against the

The first known engraving of a surfing scene appeared in 1831 in William Ellis's *Polynesian researches*.

F. Howard, Jun. del.

W. Finden, sculp.

16

belly or chest to ride prone on a wave. Because of its simplicity, belly-boarding may easily have been invented many times and at many places around the world, but there are only two areas where it was widely practised before modern times: along the shores of West Africa from Senegal to Nigeria, and along the beaches and reefs fringing the many islands of the Pacific. African surfing seems to have been independently developed by the water-loving Africans living along the Atlantic shores of that continent, though it never seems to have evolved much further than belly-boarding, or to have spread to other peoples. But the Pacific Island version of surfing presents an entirely different story.

Although it is impossible to say exactly when man first began to surf in the Pacific, the wide distribution of the sport throughout the islands of this vast ocean indicates a considerable antiquity for the sport. It probably dates as far back as three or four thousand years ago

An engraving from *Incidents of a Whaling Voyage*, by F. A. Olmsted published in 1841.

An engraving from Henry Cheever's *Life in the Sandwich Islands*, published in New York in 1851.

According to legend the wahines of early
Hawaii were just as clever in the
surf as the men. It is easy to see where
other legends, of mermaids, might
have originated.

In any Hawaiian village, the surfboard was a prized possession. In Freycinet's *Voyage Around The World* published in 1819 this engraving appeared. It depicted the houses of Kalaimoku a Hawaiian Chieftain, with the surfboard dominating the front yard.

The beauty of Hawaiian women surfers delighted many a European visitor, including Jacques Arago who sketched this maiden (below) around 1819. The missionaries who arrived the following year, soon put a stop to this kind of display.

when the ancestors of the present-day Pacific Islanders were sailing from the shores of South Asia and surrounding archipelagos out into the Pacific to discover and settle new lands. Practically everywhere these maritime people settled—from, for example, the north coast of New Guinea to tiny Easter Island off the South American coast—there is evidence of a presumably ancient surfing tradition. Surfing skills varied among the Pacific Island populations, however. Along the shores of New Guinea and the other islands of Melanesia, and on the islands of Micronesia and those of the western half of Polynesia, surfing remained in the simple belly-boarding stage. Boards were usually just a few feet long—only big enough to allow a surfer to ride prone—and typically only children and youths surfed. It was among the main islands of East Polynesia —New Zealand, Tahiti, the Marquesas and Hawaii—that longer boards were developed and the sport became something more than just a casual recreation of the younger set. In Tahiti, for example, the first explorers found that Tahitians of all ages and social classes were enthusiastic and skilful surfers, and that mature men and women prided themselves on their surfing prowess. Captain

Captain James Cook discovered the Hawaiian Islands in 1778. Among the Islanders who paddled out to welcome him was at least one man on a surfboard. This early engraving shows a surfboard rider in the foreground, left of centre. (see inset)

An early engraving showing the Hawaiians at sport.

Another early engraving which helped to introduce the old world to the pastimes of the new.

Surfing's 18th Century Peak

Dimensions of Hawaiian surfboards.

These ancient Hawaiian surfboards are in the Bishop Museum, Honolulu. They average 18 feet in length and weigh over 100 pounds.

William Bligh was able to watch Tahitian surfing first-hand when he anchored the *Bounty* at Matavai Bay on his ill-fated expedition to gather breadfruit in Tahiti, and wrote the following description of Tahitian surfing in his log:

'The heavy surf which has run on the shore for a few days past has given great amusement to many of the Natives, but is such as one would suppose would drown any European. The general plan of this diversion is for a number of them to advance with their paddles to where the Sea begins to break and placing the broad part under the Belly holding the other end with their Arms extended full length, they turn themselves to the surge and balancing themselves on the Paddles are carried to the shore with the greatest rapidity.'

Although it is not clear from Bligh's description how large the Tahitian boards, or 'paddles' as he called them, were, or in which position the Tahitians rode their boards, another early observer indicates that Tahitian surfing was considerably advanced in terms of boards and riding positions. James Morrison, the boatswain's mate on the *Bounty* who was stranded for several years on Tahiti after the mutineers took over the ship and sailed away to exile on Pitcairn Island, makes it clear in his description of Tahitian surfing that boards might be longer than a few feet in length, and that a few of the Tahitian experts were able to stand at least momentarily on their boards. These Tahitian surfing experts had their counterparts among the men who excelled at surfing in New Zealand and the Marquesas island groups where a similar trend towards the development of larger boards and more sophisticated surfing techniques was evident. But none of these Polynesian surfers from south of the Equator could ever have challenged the surfing champions of Hawaii who rode standing up on full-size surfboards and mastered the waves as no other Polynesians or other Pacific Islanders ever had.

Why surfing reached its peak in Hawaii is

Impressed by the skill the Hawaiian maidens showed in the surf, Mark Twain says that he 'tried surf bathing once, subsequently, but made a failure of it. I got the board placed right, and at the right moment, too; but missed the connection myself. The board struck the shore in three-quarters of a second, without any cargo, and I struck the bottom about the same time, with a couple barrels of water in me.'

An early painting of an Hawaiian girl riding a surfboard in the pre-missionary days.

The world's largest collection of ancient surfboards reposes in the Bishop Museum in Honolulu.

By the end of the 19th century when this photograph was taken surfing was at its lowest ebb. This lone Hawaiian surfer at Waikiki carries one of the last *alaia* boards to be ridden there.

Old redwood boards in use around 1910, now in the Bishop Museum in Honolulu.

open to conjecture. The Hawaiian environment was probably crucial, for when the first settlers came to Hawaii from the Marquesas around 750 A.D., and then from Tahiti a few hundred years later, they undoubtedly found—as do modern surfers today—that the islands have some of the finest surfing conditions in the world. The water is warm, the coastline— studded with submerged reefs, rocky headlands and sandy beaches—is ideal for forming rideable waves, and the island chain lies across the path of ocean swells that move across the Pacific year round. During Hawaii's summer, Southern Hemisphere storms from as far away as the Antarctic Sea send up powerful swells to strike Hawaii's southern shores and form the long, regular waves characteristic of surfing beaches like Waikiki. Then, during Hawaii's

26

Two *alaia* board riders on an Hawaiian
beach.

About 1907, Europeans coming to Hawaii
began enjoying the water sports.

winter, huge swells from the raging storms of the closer North Pacific storm centres fan down towards Hawaii to strike its northern shores and form the giant waves of such famous 'big-wave' breaks as those at Sunset Beach and Waimea Bay. Perhaps these ideal conditions explain why Hawaiians channelled so much of their energy into wave-riding and developed surfing into the elaborate sport that amazed its first European witnesses.

Whatever are the reasons, there is no doubt that the Pacific surfing movement had reached its peak development in Hawaii when Captain James Cook first 'discovered' the islands in 1778. Hawaiians were then using surfboards of all sizes and types. They rode them prone, kneeling or standing up, and moved with ease across the waves, twisting and turning to get the best possible ride. Their skill moved Lieutenant James King, in the official account of Cook's

Not only the Hawaiian canoe became popular with these early European visitors to the Islands . . .

. . . the surfboard also was taken up, as this early picture, taken around 1907, shows — Europeans with Hawaiian boards and a Hawaiian canoe on Waikiki beach.

From the Archives of Hawaii, this is
credited with being the first photograph
of a board rider in action.

voyage, to exclaim that 'the boldness and address with which I saw them perform these difficult and dangerous manoeuvres was altogether astonishing and is scarcely to be believed'. Other early observers were equally impressed by what they called the Hawaiians' 'favourite amusement', 'national pastime' or 'national sport', and one of them wrote that the Hawaiian love of surfing was such that when the sea offered a sudden run of good waves 'the thatch houses of a whole village stood empty', and 'daily tasks as farming,

By 1911 surfing was increasing in popularity to the point where it could support a magazine. Alexander Hume Ford began Hawaii's Magazine the *Paradise of the Pacific* in January 1911. This picture, one of the earliest published surfing photographs, decorated the back cover of the magazine.

fishing and tapa-making were left undone while the entire community—men, women and children—enjoyed themselves in the rising surf and rushing white water'.

Surfing in ancient Hawaii was not confined to a handful of favourite surfing areas, as many a modern surfer who visits the islands and goes to only the well-known breaks might suppose. The ancient Hawaiians were a coastal people, and wherever they lived along the shore they tried to surf. Evidence that Hawaiians surfed all around the coasts of the seven main islands

The surfing belle of the turn of the century was—thanks to Queen Victoria—a long way divorced from 'Venus Arising'.

European surfers in action at Waikiki, around 1915.

—Niihau, Kauai, Oahu, Molokai, Maui, Lanai and Hawaii—comes from the many reports of surfing activity left by the first explorers and other early observers, and from Hawaiian legends and chants which mention the famous surfing breaks of old. A study of these accounts and traditions resulted in a list of some 106 documented surfing breaks around the islands. Since many surfs were probably unnoticed by the first European visitors, or were not famous enough to be recorded in traditions, and since many traditions that probably contained information about surfing have not survived into modern times, the actual number of areas where Hawaiians surfed was probably several times the documented number.

Before Queen Victoria the intrepid bather wore first of all nothing and later the scantiest—for the period— costume. In the 1840s French women, naturally the most uninhibited of all, wore costumes such as these.

In the early 1900s the Canadian Costume claimed a vote for women. It was brief and baggy and all-concealing, until it shrank. Then it became so form-fitting as to be lascivious—at least in that age.

The bathing machine was pulled into the sea by a usually ancient horse. While the dragging operation was going on the bather changed into his or her neck-to-knee inside the cabin ready to take one or two quick dips before being hauled ashore again.

Despite the strictures on dress, mixed bathing was frowned on in the early days of surfing. The only accepted form of taking the waters at one period was the bathing machine. Invented in England in the 1870s the bathing machine spread across the world and the picture shows them in use at Coogee Beach near Sydney in the 1880s. The enclosure of wire in front of the machine was designed to be sharkproof. Presumably it was also manproof.

Much of the evidence on ancient Hawaiian surfing comes from the island of Hawaii, the largest and, in pre-European days, the most populous island of the chain. Almost half the known surfing breaks are located there, and most of them are clustered along the Kona coast on the southwest side of the island, a population centre of ancient Hawaii. There, along rocky shores which would daunt many a modern surfer, are found some of the famous surfing breaks of Hawaiian history: Kamoa, Kawa and Pu'u of Keolonāhihi Bay where

Early surfing in Anglo Saxon countries was not surfing at all. It was more a day by the sea as depicted in this engraving of the scene at Manly Beach, Sydney, on a public holiday in 1869.

Coogee Beach at the turn of the century with its bathing machines and absence of free swimmers in the surf.

In England, the birthplace of the bathing machine, the contraptions were much in vogue. There were 57 bathing machines on Hastings Beach, England, alone.

Kamehameha,* the first king of Hawaii, learned to surf; Kalapu and Kaulu of Keauhou Bay, famed as a site for surfing contests; and Kapahukapu, Kapukapu and Kukui at Kealakekua Bay where Captain Cook was killed in 1779 when he attempted to take a high chief hostage. It was at Kealakekua Bay that Cook and his party got a close look at surfing, and it is from there that the first published account of Hawaiian surfing, written by Lieutenant James King, comes: 'Whenever, from stormy weather or any extraordinary swell at sea the impetuosity of the surf is increased to its utmost heights, they choose that time for their amusement, which

* To say Hawaiian words correctly care must be taken to pronounce the glottal stop that frequently occurs before or between vowels, and to distinguish between long and short vowels. Here glottal stops are indicated with a ' and long vowels with a - over the vowel for all Hawaiian words except those which are so obsolete that their pronunciation has been forgotten, and except for the names of the main islands and places which are commonly written without these symbols. The main islands should be rendered as Ni'ihau, Kaua'i, O'ahu, Moloka'i, Maui, Lana'i and Hawai'i, and well known places as Lahaina and Waikiki should be written in the above form to indicate proper pronunciation.

With something like 12,000 miles of beach-studded coastline, Australia was a natural habitat for the surfer. But such were the customs of the times that the beaches went unused, except for the stroll along the sands and the occasional very discreet paddle.

While the authorities presiding over the rules and regulations applying on Australian beaches made this law and that as to what the bather could wear, the bathers themselves made more or less their own rules. This picture on a Sydney beach in the early 1900s shows the women, hats intact, showing far more leg than was decent for the times, while three teenage boys challenge the surf absolutely naked.

is performed in the following manner: Twenty or thirty of the natives, taking each a long narrow board, rounded at the ends, set out together from the shore. The first wave they meet they plunge under, suffering it to roll over them, rise again beyond it, and make the best of their way, by swimming out into the sea. The second wave is encountered in the same manner as the first; . . . as soon as they have gained by these repeated efforts, the smooth water beyond the surf, they lay themselves at

The surf bathing of the 1900s was a long way from the surfing-in-effect. This intrepid family was typical of the surf bathers of the time.

Manly Beach near Sydney was the scene of many firsts in the formative years of surfing. For some reason the populace found it irresistible to paddle in the Manly foam while most other beaches saw no one attempting the waters.

At Bondi and Coogee both, the carnival atmosphere was created on the shore and people had their fun without having to go near the neighbouring water. Nor did they have to remove any clothing. At left is William Anderson's wonderland city at Bondi, and above, all the fun of the fair at Coogee in the early 1900s.

length on their board, and prepare for their return. As the surf consists of a number of waves, of which every third is remarked to be always much larger than the others, and to flow higher on the shore, the rest breaking in the intermediate space, their first object is to place themselves on the summit of the largest surge. . . . If by mistake they should place themselves on one of the smaller waves, which breaks before they reach the land, or should not be able to keep their plank in a proper direction on the top of the swell, they are left exposed to the fury of the next, and, to avoid it, are obliged again to dive and regain their place, from which they set out. Those who succeed in their object of reaching shore, have still the greatest danger to encounter. The coast being guarded by a chain of rocks, with, here and there, a small opening between them, they are obliged to steer their boards through one of these, or, in case of failure, to quit it, before they reach the rocks, and, plunging

Such was the foreign nature of the surf. While the Pacific Ocean rolls in on magnificent Manly Beach only 50 yards away, the entrepreneurs of the turn of the century were able to make money from contrived water sports. At Manly this costly contraption was built to give the tightly-buttoned-up citizenry at least a look at the fun to be had from plunging into the waters.

Coogee Beach

The allure of the beach began to take effect. At Coogee Beach near Sydney in the early 1900s the public came down to sit on the sands for a 'family day'. Few entered the water, but the feeling was there. They were getting closer.

under the waves, make the best of their way back again. This is reckoned very disgraceful, and is also attended with the loss of the board, which I have seen, with great horror, dashed to pieces, at the very moment the islander quitted it.'

Among the early European visitors to Hawaii who were impressed by surfing and who took care to describe it at some length was the English missionary William Ellis. Ellis, who travelled from Tahiti to Hawaii at the request of the newly-arrived American missionaries who needed his expert advice on how to commence missionary work among the Hawaiians, made a complete circuit, on foot and by canoe, of the island of Hawaii in 1823 and thus had an excellent opportunity to view surfing activity all around that island's shore. 'To a spectator,' wrote Ellis, 'nothing can appear more daring, and sometimes alarming, than to see a number of persons splashing about among the waves of the sea as they dash on the shore; yet this is the most popular and

Bondi Beach in 1901 was a piece of relatively unspoiled coastline, but Sydneysiders flocked to it. Forbidden by law to enter the water in daylight hours they sat, they watched, they promenaded, while their children waded at the water's edge.

William Gocher, editor of a minor suburban newspaper at Manly, Australia, struck the first blows in the campaign to release the magnificent Australian beaches to the public. He announced in his newspaper that he would swim during forbidden hours, did so, and got away with it. Thus he opened the doors to surfers in their hundreds and thousands all over the country.

Mass Exodus to the Beaches

Men were first into the surf, but the women soon followed. Segregated bathing was the order of the day. Considering the costumes the women had to wear, it was doubtful if the females ever protested such segregation. The picture is of the costume in vogue in Australia at the turn of the century.

What to wear to the waters became fashion news in the 1900s. This outfit was described as a 'striking bathing suit of khaki-kool silk combined with black satin. It is unique, and a pleasant costume for any sort of water sport. The cap being of the same material as the suit'.

After William Gocher lead the way there was a mass exodus to the beaches. The sandhills behind the ocean became cluttered with homes and shops, the beaches crowded with people, half of them sightseers, the other half intrepid surfers. The move into the ocean had begun.

delightful of the native sports. Sometimes they choose,' Ellis continued, 'a place where the deep water reaches to the beach, but generally prefer a part where the rocks are ten or twenty feet under water, and extend to a distance from the shore, as the surf breaks more violently on these. When playing in these places, each individual takes his board, and, pushing it before him, swims perhaps a quarter of a mile or more out to sea. They do not attempt to go over the billows which roll towards the shore, but watch their approach, and dive under water, allowing the billow to pass over their heads. When they reach the outside of the rocks, where the waves first break, they adjust themselves on one end of the board, lying flat on their faces, and watch the approach of the largest billow; they then poise themselves on its highest edge, and, paddling as it were with their hands and feet, ride on the crest of the wave, in the midst of the spray and foam, till within a yard or two of the rocks on the shore; and when the

Page 41 and above.

The women of the time enjoyed the new emancipation of briefer clothing as much as the refreshment of the surf itself. The bathing belle was born in the early 1900s, shaking off for a few hours in a week the discreetness of dress imposed upon her by the morality of Queen Victoria. At the beach she found freedom, and a pride in her body. Beach fashions became very important. As awkward, as untidy, even as unshapely as the women in these pictures appear to be, they were daring for their time, and pleased to be so.

observers would expect to see them dashed to pieces, they steer with great address between the rocks, or slide off their board in a moment, grasp it by the middle, and dive under water, while the wave rolls on, and breaks among the rocks with a roaring noise, the effect of which is greatly heightened by the shouts and laughter of the natives in the water. Those who are expert frequently change their position on the board, sometimes sitting and sometimes standing erect in the midst of the foam. The greatest address is necessary in order to keep on the edge of the wave: for if they get too forward, they are sure to be overturned; and if they fall back, they are buried beneath the succeeding billow. To see,' Ellis concludes, 'fifty or a hundred persons riding on an immense billow, half emersed in spray and foam, for a distance of several hundred yards together, is one of the most novel and interesting sports a foreigner can witness in the islands.'

Surfing was called by the Hawaiians *he'e nalu,* which literally means 'wave (*nalu*) -sliding (*he'e*).' The Hawaiians had an extensive vocabulary for wave types, surfing styles and surfboards. A long wave was, for example, a *lauloa*; a low, but unbreaking wave, a'*ōhū*; and a fast curling wave a *kākala*. To surf the rider first paddled, *hoe*, out to where the surf lined up, the *kūlana nalu*. He then waited for a good wave, preferably a *nalu ha'i lala*, a 'wave that breaks diagonally', so that after paddling to catch the wave he could slide shoreward at an angle in front of the curl, a

A discreet plunge in a private pool at Little Coogee.

technique called *lala*. A surfboard was a *papa he'e nalu*, a 'plank for wave-sliding', and the surfer had two main types of board to choose from, the short, thin *alaia*, and the long, narrow, *olo*. Each, as we shall see, was adapted to a particular type of surf and demanded a particular style of surfing.

As the first migrants to Hawaii, and their Hawaii-born descendants, began to concentrate their sporting energy on surfing, they developed boards that were larger and more finely designed than the short, simple belly-boards used elsewhere in Polynesia and the Pacific. They evolved the first true surfboards that allowed riders to stand and manoeuvre at will on the slope of a wave. The two main types of Hawaiian surfboards, the *alaia* and

Surfing was for the brave, the adventurous, and the perils were many. Note in the advertisement that no mention is made of sunburn to the back, the stomach or the legs. These parts were discreetly covered.

The rush to the surf was in one way a rush to tragedy. The surf was boisterous and ever changing, with rips and currents to trap the unwary. In their voluminous costumes bathers were a ready prey to undertows and dumping waves and the rescue equipment of the day was rudimentary in the extreme. This picture was taken in 1928 depicting what might have happened at the turn of the century to the intrepid surfer.

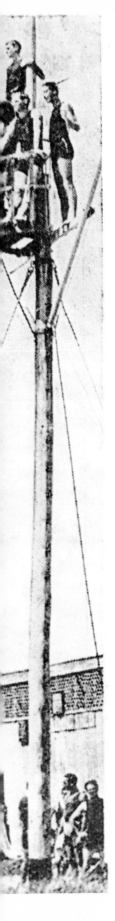

At other Australian beaches, other methods of life-saving were introduced. Cronulla plumped for a horse-driven guardian. There is no record of any rescues he may have made, with or without his horse.

With deaths from drowning increasing as the number of surf bathers increased, the methods of the British-based Life Saving Society were employed on Australian beaches. One of the Life Saving Societies' recommendations was a central tower on the beach which could be used as a look-out point and from which rescue lines could be run. The central pole idea was found to be of little use in Australia—particularly when most bathers surfed in spots as far from the centre of the beach as possible, and well out of reach of rescue lines.

Since surfing for the white man began in Manly, Australia, it was natural that the first deaths among surfers should occur there and the first methods of life-saving on the beaches should originate there. Fishing boats were used at first, particularly this one, owned by the Sly Brothers. It became the forerunner of the modern Australian surf boat.

By 1910 a handful of volunteer Surf Life
Saving Clubs had been formed and the
unique organization, the Surf Life Saving
Association of Australia, was under way.
This Association was to spread its
influence around the world for more than
the next half century. In that time it
radically improved on its dress and the
techniques apparent in this picture of the
Bronte Surf Life Saving Club of 1909.

Temporary headquarters of the Maroubra
Surf Life Saving Club.

The Surf Life Saving Club

Manly had one of the first Surf Life Saving Clubs in the world and its Rescue and Resuscitation team comprised some of the strongest swimmers in the world at that time: at rear, left to right, Arthur Relph, Jack Taylor; front row, left to right, Bill Kellam, Gus Tartakover, George Robey, and world 100 yards freestyle record holder, Cecil Healy.

the *olo*, were thus the result of hundreds of years of experimentation and testing by generations of Hawaiians to develop boards suited for maximum performance in the surfing breaks around their islands.

The *alaia* boards remained closest to the original belly-boards in that they were fairly short, thin and probably could not fully support a rider until the board was planing on a wave. An average *alaia* board was perhaps six to eight feet long, fourteen to eighteen inches wide and an inch or so thick. The nose was usually wide and rounded, and the sides tapered towards a squared-off tail. In cross-section, both decks were apparently convex, meeting with narrow and sometimes sharp siderails.

Although some observers reported *olo* boards twenty-four feet in length, most were probably in the fourteen to eighteen-foot range. The

47

Early Ages: Flagellation Method

Whipping with stinging nettles, later supplemented by striking the skin surfaces with the hands and wet cloths, was considered helpful in restoring those apparently in deep sleep by inflicting pain.

1530: Bellows Method

Paracelsus was first to use common fireside bellows to introduce air into lungs of apparently dead persons. Adaptations of this were used through Europe for 300 years.

So-called 'civilized' man was a non-swimmer. He seldom ventured near the water and even the majority of sailors could not swim. So little was known of the techniques of resuscitating the apparently drowned and some of the methods employed were quite barbaric, as these pictures show.

board once owned by the high chief Paki— a magnificent board that was probably surfed at Waikiki in the 1830s and which is now on display at the Bishop Museum in Honolulu —is probably representative of the *olo* type. It is nearly sixteen feet long, slightly over eighteen inches across at its widest point, six inches thick, and weighs around one hundred and sixty pounds. Like the *alaia*, it has a wide nose, a squared-off tail and convex decks. But the great length and thickness of the board

overwhelm these similarities and give Paki's *olo*, and all other known *olo* boards, a long, cigar-shaped appearance that contrasts markedly with that of the thin, plank-like *alaia* boards. Although the wood of the breadfruit and other common trees was often used for making surfboards, wood from the mahogany-like *koa* trees and the balsa-like *wiliwili* trees—trees that were also prized for making canoe hulls, and canoe outrigger floats, respectively—was apparently favoured by boardmakers and

1773: Barrel Method

Used prior to 1767. May still be seen along water front. Barrel movement forward released pressure on victim's chest allowing inspiration. Movement of barrel back caused body's weight to compress chest, inducing expiration.

The inversion method—pressure over the chest aided in expelling air from lungs and inspiration resulted when pressure was removed. Many successful cases of resuscitation from drowning were recorded.

1812 . . . Trotting Horse Method

Used on Europe's inland waterways for resuscitation from drowning. Victim's body contacting horse, compressed his chest, forcing out air. When he was bounced from horse's back, his chest expanded and air entered lungs.

surfers. Expert boardmakers were employed to search the forests for sound trees which were then felled and shaped on the spot into one or more rough surfboard blanks. A roughed-out blank would then be hauled down to the shore for finishing in a canoe house or some other suitable structure. Careful work with fine adzes and coral sanding blocks gave the board its final shape, and polishing with stone rubbers gave it its smooth finish. The board was then stained a dark colour with one or more

49

Bondi was the first beach to sport a recognized Surf Life Saving Club—here pictured in 1906. It was at Bondi that the surf reel, now an essential part of the equipment of Life Saving organizations on beaches all over the world, originated. Pictured is one of Bondi's—and the world's—first reels with the old-fashioned and cumbersome—indeed dangerous—cork-fllled life belts on the lifesaver in the centre front row.

Australia introduced the Schafer method of artificial resuscitation to cope with the emergencies it was experiencing amongst novice bathers on its boisterous beaches. Volunteer Clubs that mushroomed between 1906 and 1912 were not all confined to men. Wollongong formed the first Women's Rescue and Resuscitation team in the world and if it did not last for long it was at least interesting—particularly since the uniform of the lady lifesavers seems today to have been designed to make the girls themselves candidates for drowning.

vegetable dyes. When the stain was dry a dressing of *kukui* nut oil or cocoa-nut oil was applied to give it a black, glossy finish and make it ready for surfing.

The finished product was a highly valued possession among the Hawaiians. Boards were cared for by drying and oiling them after each surfing session, and then by wrapping them in tapa cloth and suspending them inside a house to keep the boards from being damaged by the sun or insects.

Highly manoeuvreable *alaia* boards were adapted for catching steep, fast-breaking *kākala*

waves, and for the *lala* technique of riding diagonally across the wave's face. Although they lacked the tail-fin modern surfers consider so essential for top performance, *alaia* boards could apparently be turned at will and ridden across a wave with ease. An eyewitness to a Hawaiian surfing a seven-foot board at Hilo on the island of Hawaii described a typical *alaia* ride:

'One instantly dashed in, in front of and at the lowest declivity of the advancing wave, and . . . established his position; then without further effort shot along the base of the wave eastward with incredible velocity . . . his course was along

A women's Rescue and Resuscitation team was also formed at Coogee in 1911 and at Manly. The photograph of the Manly R and R team taken during a Surf Carnival on Manly Beach in 1914 shows that the women on the Australian beaches were gradually becoming more emancipated in their dress.

The first European to body surf—Fred Williams of the Manly, N.S.W., Club. As a youth he learned the art from Tommy Tanna, a Polynesian working in Manly as a gardener.

The early Australian Surf Life Saving Clubs were very much voluntary organizations, receiving little or no help from local authorities. The clubs organized their own forms of protest against this official inactivity and failure to provide funds for the equipment that would save lives on the beaches under the various local council jurisdictions.

the foot of the wave, and parallel to it . . . so as soon as the bather had secured his position he gave a spring and stood on his knees upon the board, and just as he was passing us . . . he gave another spring and stood upon his feet, now folding his arms on his breast, and now swinging them about in wild ecstasy in his exhilarating ride.'

The giant *olo* boards were designed for massive but slower-breaking surf and for long rides. Their great length, narrowness and buoyancy enabled the surfer to pick up a wave long before it became steep enough to break, and to ride it all the way to the beach long after the wave had crested and lost most of its power. *Olo* boards were therefore ideal for the

By 1912 the Surf Life Saving movement on the Sydney beaches was well established and the various clubs participated in regular surf carnivals that drew crowds of up to 30,000 each Saturday during the summer season. Below is the scene at Manly Surf Life Saving Club's first carnival on January 6th, 1912. A crowd of 20,000 attended.

Very quickly the Australian lifesaver
became a kind of super-hero. He was seen
at his best at the surf carnivals in the
colourful march pasts and the Rescue and
Resuscitation drills. The picture shows
the Bondi club march past at a Manly
carnival in 1909. The belt man is wearing
the outmoded cork-filled belt, and all the
lifesavers the 'proper' dress of the time,
which had to cover the chest, then extend
down the thighs to the pair of 'vees'.
At that the lifesavers were breaking the
existing regulations which required that
the body be covered from the neck to
the knee, including the upper arms.

long-breaking surf at gently sloping beaches
like Waikiki. But their great bulk made turns
and other manoeuvres difficult, so that they
were not suited to rocky shores and steep,
quick-breaking surf. Since most of the surfing
areas of ancient Hawaii were of this latter type,
it is not surprising that *alaia* surfing dominates
in the early accounts of the sport (all the
descriptions of surfing quoted here have been
of *alaia*-type surfing) and that more *alaia* than
olo boards are represented in museum
collections.

This contrast between *olo* and *alaia* boards and
styles of surfing also figures in Hawaiian social

The women were not to be outdone. If the men were to be the super-heroes of the surf, the Australian woman was going to make her play. The fashions of the time were against her, but she pressed on in joining her own life saving groups within the clubs, and her own swimming clubs such as this one at the Sydney Domain Baths in 1907.

In less than a dozen years surf bathing, from being a prohibited activity became a social event. At the Manly Surf Club Carnival in January, 1908, thousands of spectators swarmed the beach and the surrounding cliffs to watch the men take to the waters.

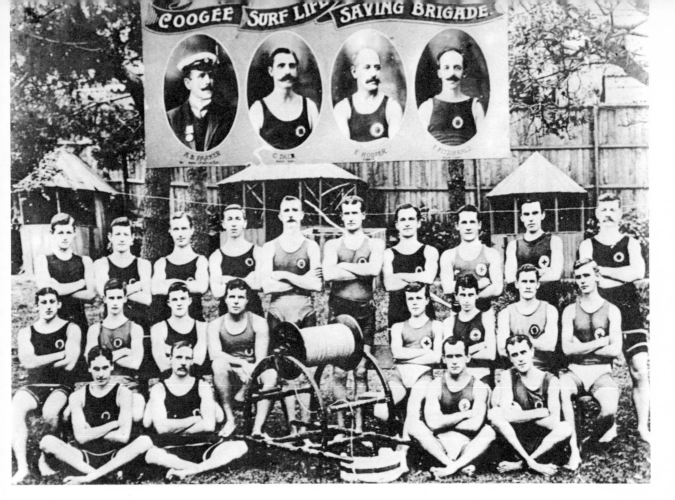

The hero image attracted the strongest and fittest into the Surf Life Saving movement and the clubs became stronger and more organized. The Coogee club around 1911.

The lifesavers themselves were aware of their hero image. At the strong Manly club, in 1916, lifesavers took their popular description of 'blonde Vikings' literally.

structure. Chiefs, or *ali'i* and commoners, or *maka'āinana*, were rigidly divided in Hawaiian society, and it appears that *olo* boards were primarily used by the chiefs, if not exclusively reserved for them. In addition, there is evidence that chiefs could tabu a surfing beach to commoners and that the latter were seldom, if ever, allowed to ride with chiefs. The missionary Ellis remarked, ' . . . that when the king or queen, or any high chiefs are playing [in the surf], none of the common people are allowed to approach these places, lest they spoil their sport.'

Expertise apparently accompanied privilege, for chiefly surfers were noted for their prowess on the waves. Ellis states that 'The chiefs pride themselves much in excelling in some of the games of the country; hence Taumuarii, the late king of Taui [Kauai] was celebrated as the most expert swimmer in the surf, known in the islands.' Instruction in surfing was part of a young chief's education, and he derived much strength and stamina from this and other aristocratic sports. King Kamehameha I, the high chief who conquered all of Hawaii and founded a dynasty in the early years of contact

57

with Europeans, had been especially trained
to surf in his youth, and was particularly famed
for his skill in a variation of surfing called
lele wa'a. In *lele wa'a* a surfer leaped with his
board from a moving canoe onto a cresting
wave, and surfed it to shore, a formidable
manoeuvre when you consider that a chief's
board might weigh well over 100 pounds.
Enthusiasm for such surfing feats was
apparently not confined to young chiefs, for
Ellis says he saw ' . . . Karaimoku and Kakioeva,
some of the highest chiefs in the island, both
between fifty and sixty years of age, and large
corpulent men, balancing themselves on their
narrow board, or splashing about in the foam,
with as much satisfaction as youths of sixteen.'
A chief often had a special surf chant that
boasted of his skill in the waves, and a special
retainer assigned to chant it when appropriate.
According to the legend of Naihe, a champion
surfer from the south tip of Hawaii, his chant
once served to save his life. Naihe was so expert

As the years rolled by, more and more
conventions were broken down, more and
more people wanted to use the
sun-drenched beaches. Yet many were
still reluctant to set foot in the waves.

They came at first in ones, then in twos,
then in twenties, then in hundreds. By
1928 Manly in mid-summer presented
this scene.

At Bondi, too, the carnivals were drawing
their crowds, though the great majority
were spectators only, keeping their clothes
firmly buttoned up.

The Surfing Life

By 1935 most of the taboos had broken down, the surf bathers were more relaxed, they were enjoying themselves.

The spread of the automobile brought the coastal beaches to almost everyone. In 1935, when this picture was taken, Bondi Beach was aswarm every Saturday, Sunday and public holiday.

The rush into the surf was on. Coogee Beach, 1937.

a surfer that the chiefs from the north of the island became jealous and plotted to kill him. After inviting him to a surfing match at Hilo, in their district, they secretly made the rule that no one, once he had paddled out to the breakers, could return to shore until he heard his personal chant from the beach. Although Naihe had brought his personal chanter with him to the contest, he allowed the old woman to fall asleep while he paddled out to join the other chiefs in the surf. Once he reached the break, however, he learned of the secret rule and realized he was marooned at sea. Fortunately a friendly chief decided to aid Naihe and sent a servant to wake the old woman. With tears streaming down her cheeks,

Oh, to be in England now that the life-savers—the men, not the lollies—are there!

LAUNCHING OF THE FIRST ENGLISH SURF LIFE-SAVING TEAM.

HUH!
LIFESAVER!!
WATER GIGOLO!!!

COAST
GUARD

AUSTRALIA

English professional life-saver speaks his jealous mind.

The lifesavers were not overtaken by their image. They worked hard and kept themselves magnificently fit. Above is the first Australian team of lifesavers to compete overseas, in 1939, in Honolulu.

The reputation of the bronzed god-like lifesaver of the Australian beaches spread overseas, along with the Australian developed principles of volunteer life saving. As these cartoons show, the first visit of Australian lifesavers to England in 1935 created an enormous impression.

she rushed down to the beach to chant the words that would allow her master to return to shore:

> The day is a rough one, befitting Naihe's
>   surfboard,
> He leaps in, he swims, he strides out to the
>   waves,
> The waves that rush hither from Kahiki.
> White capped waves, billowy waves,
> Waves that break into a heap, waves that
>   break and spread.
> The surf rises above them all,
> The rough surf of the island,
> The great surf that pounds and thrashes . . . .

The use of surf chants lasted into the 19th century. Queen Emma had her own surf chant, as did David Kalākaua, the last king in the ill-fated Kamehameha dynasty. Kalākaua was not a skilful surfer, however, and the chant he used to boast of his glory and recall the chiefly skills of ancient Hawaii was that of Naihe who had lived centuries before him.

Surfing was not a sport for men only in ancient

61

The lifesavers' regimen was a strict one. Constant carnival competition in a dozen different events made the Australian lifesaver an example to every young man. Here one of the Australian stars, Rex Phillipps, in action in a beach sprint.

The lifesavers were constantly looking for ways of improving their techniques so that more lives might be saved. The Schafer method of artificial resuscitation was the standby, but young lifesavers were also taught the Holger-Nielsen method, as shown by these trainees at Bondi.

The Australian surfer became a strong and speedy swimmer—the equal of any in the world. 'Boy' Charlton was one Australian champion who could hold his own anywhere. He is shown here with the American swimming champion, Johnny Weismuller. Charlton, Weismuller and the Hawaiian, Duke Kahanamoku, were the greatest swimmers in the world in the 1920s.

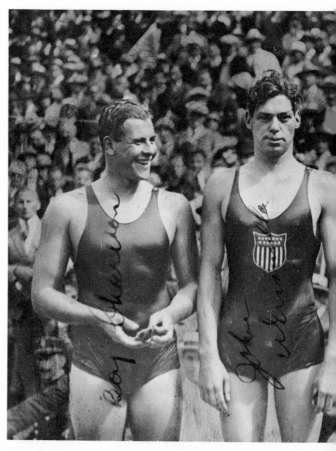

Hawaii. Women also enjoyed the waves and, according to legend, at least one surfing break—Kekaiomamala (The Sea of Mamala)—was named after a champion woman surfer. Early visitors to the islands were delighted—or shocked if they were missionaries—at the sight of comely beauties frolicking nude, or nearly nude, in the surf. It also upset the missionaries that surfing and sexual freedom went hand in hand, for as Waiamau, a Hawaiian expert on surfing lore has written, riding together on the

The Eve rocker method of resuscitation was used in acute cases of apparent drowning along Australian beaches.

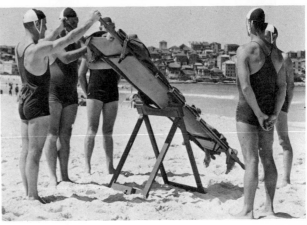

The lifesavers' methods were so effective they were incorporated into school curriculums in Australia. Here girls from a Sydney High School are undergoing examinations for their Royal Life Saving medallions.

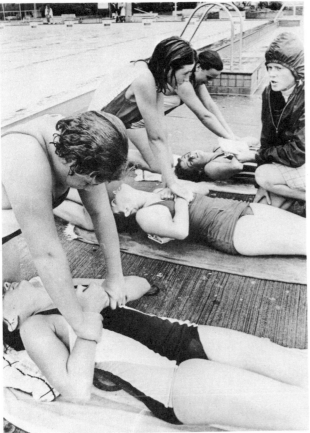

same wave might often be a prelude to sexual relations later.

Surfing was an ideal sport for showing off one's figure or physique, as well as one's athletic skill, to attract a mate. Hawaiian legends abound in stories where a future mate was first sighted surfing, or where surfing was an integral part of courtship. The high chief Moikeha is said, for example, to have first been attracted to his two wives, Ho'oipokamalani and her sister Hinau'u, when he saw them

In 1960 the mouth-to-mouth method of resuscitation was introduced, to become the standard method of reviving the apparently drowned on Australian beaches.

The Australian life saving methods spread around the world. To Ceylon . . . to Lagos . . . to Britain . . . and to Hong Kong . . . where the girls joined in, . . . and in Biarritz, France, too.

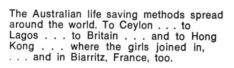

surfing at the famous curling surf of Makaiwa at Wailua on Kauai's east coast. Moikeha was returning from a long voyage to Tahiti and back when he sailed into Wailua Bay and spied the two lovely daughters of the high chief of Kauai riding the surf. Struck by their beauty, and weary of his travels, Moikeha decided to settle in Kauai and marry the two sisters. Afterwards it was said of Moikeha that his voyaging days were over and that:

> *He is dwelling at ease in Kauai,*
> *Where the surf of Makaiwa curves and bends,*
> *Where the kukui blossoms of Puna change,*
> *Where the waters of Wailua stretch out,*
> *He will live and die on Kauai.*

Kelea, a famous woman surfer from Maui, is the subject of another story linking surfing and courtship. Kelea, the beautiful sister of the ruler of Maui, was noted as the most graceful and daring surfer on the island. One day while surfing at Lahaina on the south coast she accepted an offer from an Oahu chief to ride

The Rescue and Resuscitation team was a long way from Bondi, as was the surf boat of the Ceylon Surf Life Saving Club far removed from the racers of the Sydney surf.

Australian surfers travelling abroad spread the gospel wherever they went and always made a strong appeal with their husky physique and precision drilling. These are Australian surfers introducing their techniques in Britain.

In return, Britain showed its interest. On several visits to Australia by Queen Elizabeth II and the Duke of Edinburgh, a Surf Carnival was an essential part of the celebrations arranged for the Royal tour.

Lifesavers in Biarritz, France, were taught the Australian rescue methods.

the waves in his canoe. The chief, Kalamakua, taking advantage of a squall that blew the craft out to sea, abducted Kelea and sailed with her to Oahu where he presented her as a bride to Lolale, the high chief of the island. Kelea, after her anger had cooled, accepted her lot and tried to live happily with Lolale. But Lolale disliked the sea and dwelt inland at Lihu'e. Kelea was unhappy confined at Lihu'e so far from the sea, and only found joy when she could visit the seashore and surf with her abductor, Kalamakua. Finally, she could take her exile from the sea no longer, and she left her husband to return to the shores of Maui. On her way home, however, she met Kalamakua once again and accepted a proposal of marriage from this fellow surfer.

Not every story of surfing and courtship has a happy ending, however. According to one legend, a young chief of Kauai called Kahekilani, sailed over to Oahu to prove his surfing prowess in the great waves that welled up at Pau Malū, on Oahu's north coast.

The lifesavers did a tremendous job. And never more so than on 'Black Sunday' at Bondi in February, 1938, when nearly 100 bathers were swept off a sandbank and the greatest mass rescue in the history of surfing was carried out by the patrolling lifesavers, shown above resuscitating some of the rescued.

So sound were the methods used to save lives on the Australian beaches that they changed little over the years. In this picture, lifesavers during Rescue and Resuscitation drill on a Sydney beach in 1930.

(It may surprise the modern surfer, but both Pau Malū—now called Sunset Beach—and Waimea Bay, places which are now considered to provide Hawaii's biggest and most challenging waves, were surfed by the surfing champions of ancient Hawaii.) While testing his skill in the waves at Pau Malū Kahekilani attracted the attention of the Bird Maiden, a woman of supernatural powers, who enticed him into the cave, overlooking the surf, where she lived. There he stayed for several months,

The other three pictures show the
same drill carried out in 1970.
The lifesavers' uniform is much the same
and the only obvious change is in the style
of the life belt. The cork belts were
considered to be too buoyant for diving
under the waves and the 1970 model was
a great improvement, being light and fitted
with a quick-release pin.

enchanted by her spells, until once again the
great winter surf of Pau Malū started breaking
and he was drawn back to the waves. The
Bird Maiden allowed him to leave only after
he promised not to embrace another woman.
However, the excitement of surfing clouded
Kahekilani's memory and he allowed a
beautiful woman to place an *'ilima* flower
lei around his neck and to embrace him.
He thought nothing of the incident and paddled
back to the surf, but the bird messengers of

69

Training Ground for Olympics

Bob Newbiggin was considered to be one of the greatest surf swimmers of all time, winning ten Australian titles.

The athletes in the Surf Clubs became national heroes, their feats of strength, speed and endurance acting as a magnet for thousands of youngsters who wanted nothing more than to join a surf club, carry out the voluntary work, and become heroes themselves. Robin Biddulph was aged only 16 and weighed 15½ stone in 1936-37, when he was Australian swimming champion and junior surf champion.

His huge lung capacity made 'Boy' Charlton an unusually buoyant swimmer. Here he takes a deep breath on a turn.

the Bird Maiden who saw it all flew back to tell their mistress that Kahekilani had broken his vow. When she heard the news, the Bird Maiden ran down to the beach, snatched the *'ilima lei* from Kahekilani's neck, replaced it with one made of *lehua* flowers, and ran back to her cave. Kahekilani tried to follow, but half-way up the hill he was turned to stone. Kahekilani still sits there today, although now it seems that someone has renamed him the George Washington Stone!

Hawaiian surfers were not always involved in amatory affairs; they were fiercely competitive in the waves and champion surfers vied for

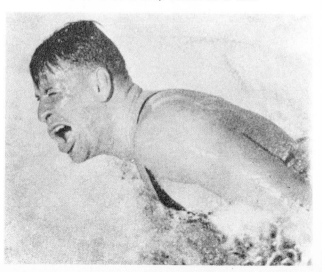

The Surf Clubs also gave the nucleus of Australia's Olympic swimming teams before World War II. Three Australian Olympic swimmers, who were heroes in America were, left to right, Harry Hay, Frank Beaurepaire and Andrew 'Boy' Charlton, shown here in the Hollywood pool of film comedian Harold Lloyd (top left) with Count Zeppo, in 1932.

'Boy' Charlton (on the right) was only a schoolboy when he was taking on the best swimmers in the world and beating them as he did in January, 1924, against Sweden's Arne Borg. This photograph was taken after the New South Wales 880 yards championship, which Charlton won by 8 yards in a world record time of 10 minutes 51 seconds.

top honours in contests around the islands. According to David Malo, a noted 19th century Hawaiian scholar, surfers competed primarily in terms of the speed and length of their rides. After paddling out to a predetermined position to await the waves, the contestants lined up and upon a signal paddled together to catch the same wave and race shorewards to be first past a buoy placed inshore. Chiefs were frequent competitors in such contests and, according to Waiamau, the surfing authority cited earlier, if the contest was one of 'pride', they would wear tapa loincloths dyed red. Chiefly contestants also often enjoyed the privilege of

71

Nowhere in the world could one find such a parade of athletes as can be found on any Sunday at one of the Sydney beach carnivals, when teams from all clubs compete against one another.
In the belt race . . .

feasting on roast dog, cooked specially for them in an earth oven, between heats so they could replenish themselves for the next round of waves.

Keauhou Bay, on the Kona coast of Hawaii, was the site of an unusual form of competition between surfers and *hōlua* sledders. At Keauhou a long stone runway, part of which can still be seen today, ran from the mountainside above the bay to the water's edge. Grass would be strewn on the runway so that the chiefs could easily slide down it on specially constructed wooden *hōlua* sleds. Opposite the end of the runway was a famous surf, and when the waves were running high there expert surfers would challenge the champion *hōlua* sledders. A surfer would take his place at the break, while a sledder would stand poised at the top of the runway. When a good wave approached a tapa cloth flag would be flashed to signal the start of the race: the sledder would give a short run and throw himself and his sled on top of the

. . . and in the surf race . . . and in beach events such as the musical flags—a race to grab sticks from the sand . . .

runway and start his rapid descent; and the surfer would start paddling to catch the wave and ride it to shore. The first man to reach a grass house on the beach at the terminus of the slide was declared the winner.

Betting, both between surfers and spectators, was an integral part of surfing contests and is said to have added much zest to the sport. According to Hawaiian authorities, stakes were often high, and might include all a man's property and his personal liberty as well.

An account of a legendary surfing contest in which 'Umi-a-Liloa, a great chief in Hawaii

. . . or the beach sprint . . .

around 1500 A.D., took part, illustrates the seriousness of surfing contests and the wagering that went with them: 'On the death of Hakau, the ruler of the island of Hawaii, his brother 'Umi, was forced to flee because of troubles in Hakau's court. When 'Umi had fled, and was living at Waipunalei, in the Hilo district, unknown and in disguise, he and his friend, Koi, attended a surf-swimming match at Laupahoehoe. A petty chief of the district, named Paiea, invited 'Umi to a match, and

offered a trifling bet, which 'Umi refused.
Paiea then offered to bet four double canoes,
and 'Umi, at the request, and being backed by
friends, accepted the bet. 'Umi won the bet,
but in coming in over the surf, by accident or
design, Paiea's surfboard struck the shoulder
of 'Umi and scratched off the skin. 'Umi said
nothing then, but when he had attained to
power and was making his first tour around
the island, on arriving at Laupahoehoe he
caused Paiea to be killed and taken up to the

the pillow fight amongst the burliest club
members . . . or one of the toughest tests
of physical strength and co-ordination,
the chariot race on the soft and yielding
sands.

Surf, Sand and Pageantry

And the most spectacularly colourful event of them all on the sands—the march past of the club teams in their colours, precision marching to the skirl of the bagpipes.

Heiau [temple] at Waipunalei to be sacrificed to his god.'

Like just about everything else in ancient Hawaii surfing had its sacred aspect. The link between surfing and ritual began the moment a tree was selected by a master boardbuilder as likely material for a surfboard. Before felling the tree, he would place a red *kumu* fish at the base of the trunk. Then, after felling the tree with stone adzes, he would dig a hole in its roots and leave the fish there as an offering to the gods in return for the tree he was about to shape into a surfboard. After roughing out the board on the site, and finishing it to perfection on the shore, another ritual—which, unfortunately, has not been recorded—had to be performed, particularly if it were a chief's board, before it was ready for the surf.

Although it is not known if there was a Hawaiian counterpart of the Tahitian god of surfing, a deity named *Huaori*, we do know that a special deity of sports, the *Akua Pa'ani*, presided over surfing contests, and that surfing was part of the semi-religious *Makahiki* celebrations. During these celebrations, which were held from mid-October through mid-January (the harvest months, and also the months of winter surf) the Hawaiians stopped work, relaxed and gave much of their time to sports, dancing and feasting. Thousands would gather to watch the great sports tournaments, in which surfing contests were prominently featured.

There is also some evidence that links surfing with Hawaiian temples, the stone *heiau* that once dotted the coastline of all the islands. Two of these temples that have surfing associations were still standing in the 1960s: *Keolonāhihi Heiau* on the south shore of the bay where Kamehameha I learned to surf; and *Kuemanu Heiau* some miles further south along the Kona coast of Hawaii. Although the exact relationship between these temples and surfing has never been fully worked out,

Little wonder that from the earliest age Australians were attracted to the Surf Life Saving movement. These are Bronte and Bondi Midgets of the 1934 and 1935 vintage.

Hawaiian residents questioned in 1906 about the *Kuemanu Heiau* said that it was a '... *heiau* for surf-riding, where they could pray for good surfing weather, and consequently good sport...' and that the stone-lined pool alongside the *heiau* was '... convenient for removing salt on return [from surfing]'. It is notable that this *heiau*, and the one at Keolonāhihi, both have long stone terraces facing surfing breaks that would appear to have been ideal for observing the surf, resting on after surfing, or for standing on while

80

praying for a good run of waves.

Although it is not specifically associated with these *heiau*, one Hawaiian surf invocation has survived in the literature. When the surf was flat, surfers would wade into the ocean carrying strands of the *pōhuehue* vine (beach morning glory), and striking the water with them, they would try to call up the surf with this chant:

> *Arise! Arise! Great surfs from Kahiki,*
> *Powerful curling waves, arise with the*
>   *Pōhuehue,*
> *Well up, long-raging surf.*

One freedom that was not available on Australian beaches was the freedom to do what one liked. Regulations of the most exacting kind governing the attire of bathers was lampooned by the lifesavers in a continuing battle that went from the turn of the century right into the early 1960s.

Women made their share of protest, too, as these costumes of the period show. They wanted the same liberties the men were taking for themselves.

The Bathing Costume

Such was the high state of surfing when the first explorers touched on Hawaii in the late 1700s. Following this 'discovery' of Hawaii, surfing began to decline rapidly from this peak of development and by the late 1800s, scarcely a hundred years after their first contacts with

In 1920 youngsters sneaked their fathers' copies of the *Police Gazette* to see 'naked ladies' in their new season's costumes.

Fanny Durack, the Australian girl who became champion swimmer of the world, caused a sensation every time she appeared, and not because of her speed in the water, but because of her 'abbreviated' costume. The picture, below left, taken in January, 1918, certainly caused a storm, but it also caused other female swimmers to want to wear fewer clothes in the water.

Placegetters in the *Sunday Times* contest, left to right, Ethel Warren, 2nd; Edith Pickup, 1st; and Dorothy Woolley, 3rd.

the outside world the Hawaiians had virtually abandoned their once national sport.

As early as the 1840s, scarcely twenty years after one visitor to the islands had described whole villages taking to the surf, another noted in a volume entitled *Scenes and Scenery of the Sandwich Islands* that surfing was coming to be a rare sight around the islands. In the 1850s a traveller visiting Hawaii wrote that Lahaina on the island of Maui was one of the few places in the islands where the people seemed to have much enthusiasm for surfing, but that even there the sport seemed to be on the wane. Twenty years later, two visitors to Hilo— perhaps the last stronghold of surfing on the island of Hawaii—reported that although

The surfers quickly got their own news sheets and magazines. This one, in 1917, featured the girl on the cover, photographed in America, in a costume so brief by Australian standards, the magazine was a sellout.

The first bathing girl contest held in Australia attracted hordes of young women. These are some of the entrants in the competition, held in February, 1920.

The nine finalists in the *Sunday Times* 'most beautiful surf girl contest', 1920.

THE SURF

A JOURNAL OF SPORT AND PASTIME

OFFICE: 16 BOND STREET.   PHONE: 8546 CITY

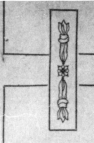

OBJECTIVE: The Development and Protection of our Beaches

No. 1   SYDNEY: SATURDAY, DECEMBER 1, 1917.   PRICE ONE PENNY.

About Ourselves

This paper is a paper with an object. Its object is to get sold. Its price is one penny per copy; but, as we are anxious to secure a large circulation, any one can have twelve copies for one shilling.

Seriously, the object of "The Surf" is to champion the interests of the beaches and work steadily for their protection and development.

The pages of "The Surf" will be open to the members of the public and surfing clubs to ventilate their grievances and defend their rights.

"The Surf" does not forget that the surfer is a gay-hearted, care-free child of Nature, who enjoys the good things the gods have given him, and it will, therefore, strive to reflect in its pages some of the gladness that dwells in their hearts.

Surf Shooters & Sirens

Buy a copy of "The Surf"—don't borrow it.

   * * *

Yes! We know that we are kicking off at a bad time, thank you!

   * * *

To Martin Brennan, Will Lawless, Joe Smith, Dick Gilbert, and others—many thanks for kind wishes.

   * * *

To the public—we guarantee to be honest.

It's the best policy. Ask our religious editor. He's had a go at both.

   * * *

Two Con's we don't want—Consumption and the other.

   * * *

Tom Taylor says that if ever they put his name in "The Surf" he'll bolt the editor of this paper how. Well, it's up to you, Tom!

   * * *

And it's also up to Sam Barnachy to buy himself a new bathing costume.

He says he's going to buy one—but when?—

When Australia is free from the rabbit and brumbies abound on the Quay;

When the tote shops in Sydney reopen, and China has run out of tea,

When Billy Hughes sticks to his pledges, and they've fixed up the Barren Jack dam;

And a wowser turns down a cheap whisky,

He'll buy a new costume—will Sam.

   * * *

There's more good looking girls on our eastern beaches than are to be found in any other portion of the globe.

   * * *

That puts us right with the ladies.

ONE OF OUR SURFING GIRLS.

—Block kindly lent by Union Theatres, Ltd.

Tibby and Dave—the Terrible Two—reckon they are going to take a fall out of Smyth, the wrestler. We wish 'em luck.

   * * *

The lurid jems of language that the "Bondi Groper" gave vent to when the blue bottle stung him would raise the hair on an Egyptian mummy.

   * * *

The sight of a surf board is as sweet to Frank Foran as the smell of grease paint to an actor.

   * * *

Dick Morris, the soulful surfer, says that he doesn't lay claim to any knowledge of the fair sex, as he was brought up on the bottle. Well, he certainly leads the world in profanity.

   * * *

George Bibb, the pirate, was sporting in the surf last Tuesday. He looked like a bull in a pansy patch.

   * * *

So was our own Aby Soper. Light as thistle down, he was rushing shorewards on the crest of a huge dumper, but before we could reach him he disappeared in a cloud of spray and blasphemy.

   * * *

Bill Craven's new surf board shot him so high the other day that he's only just come down.

Oh, girls! Supposing he hadn't.

   * * *

From constant sun baking some of our Bondi sirens are getting blacker than a spade flush.

   * * *

The team from Bondi Junction drink so much beer that they can tell the time by the taste.

   * * *

And so do some of our week-end campers.

   * * *

All communications concerning this column must reach this office not later than Tuesday each week.

   * * *

The pride of all Australia blazed in her eyes as the Coogee pirate accosted her. "Sir," said she, "you have stone bruised your heel, and it's affected your brain pan."

   * * *

Some men are so mean that they don't like parting with their breath for nothing.

   * * *

Billie Wagland is shooting 'em well lately.

   * * *

You may talk of brave beach rangers,
And of your pirates sing,
But to sit on the beach when big Denny's about
Is the sign of an early spring.

   * * *

Little Jean Watts is the youngest surf shooter on the beach.

And she's one of the prettiest.

   * * *

Jerry Ralph—the mad musician—is getting a colour up, alright. He'll be as black as the last ball in snooker directly.

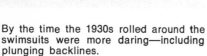

By the time the 1930s rolled around the swimsuits were more daring—including plunging backlines.

By the end of the 30s sex appeal was being accentuated in women's bathing costumes.

Hawaiians were still riding the waves there, few of the younger generation were learning to surf and that those who did were undistinguished surfers. This precipitous decline in surfing's popularity prompted Nathaniel Emerson, an expert on Hawaiian lore, to write in 1892 that: 'The sport of surf-riding possessed a grand fascination and for a time seemed as if it had the vitality of its own as a national pastime. There are those living . . . who remember the time when almost the entire population of a village would at certain hours resort to the sea-side to indulge in, or to witness, this magnificent accomplishment. We cannot but mourn its decline. But this too has felt the touch of civilization, and today it is hard to find a surfboard outside of our museums and private collections.'

The 'touch of civilization' referred to by

World War II broke down all barriers and the women achieved some kind of equality—at least on the beaches. The Manly club in Sydney formed a ladies' march past team which considerably swelled attendances at Surf Carnivals.

Today the Australian beaches, along with beaches all over the world, feature the ultimate in exposure.

The Shark Menace

They want to swim, but they are not going to. Out there, just off shore, is the unmistakable dorsal fin of a shark.

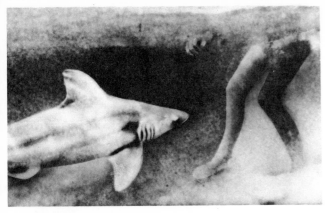

The two main dangers facing the surfers were shark attacks and drowning. Shark attacks were particularly prevalent on the Eastern Australian coast until meshing of the main beaches was introduced in 1937. This amazing picture of a shark swimming near an unsuspecting swimmer was taken inside Sydney Harbour in 1969.

Emerson was hardly lightly felt by the Hawaiians. Between Cook's visit in 1778 and 1900, the population dropped from an estimated 300,000 to less than 40,000—a figure which by then included part as well as pure Hawaiians. The long-isolated Hawaiians had virtually no natural immunity to epidemic diseases carried by Europeans, and even childhood diseases like the measles killed them in the tens of thousands.

This period of population decline was also a time of great social, economic and political upheaval in the islands. First, Kamehameha—originally just a high chief, and, as we have previously mentioned, a great surfer of the island of Hawaii—used European arms and advisers to help him conquer all the islands and found a kingdom. Then, in 1819, under the impact of alien ideas and new political realities, Kamehameha's heir declared an end to the

The shark bell is a familiar sight on Australian beaches, its pealing is a signal for surfers to flee from the water as a shark has been sighted.

kapu, or tabu system so important to regulating Hawaiian social and religious life. A year later American missionaries landed and, stepping into a spiritual vacuum, within a generation managed to convert many Hawaiians to Christianity. Traders seeking scented sandalwood that once grew in profusion in the Hawaiian forests, and whalers seeking supplies, recreation and women, further disrupted Hawaiian life in the first half of the century. In the second half of the century, when the

Intensive studies have been made of the sharks' habits, but there is still no complete answer as to why sharks attack man, or how such attacks can be prevented.

One of the early forms of shark protection in Australia, a suspended net at Coogee Beach erected in 1937. It collapsed the same year.

90

effects of population decline became more evident, further pressures from outsiders were felt by the Hawaiians. Americans and other foreign settlers came to dominate commerce in the islands and to take up much of the land in the kingdom. Soon they were importing boatloads of Chinese and Japanese labourers (since the Hawaiians were by then too few in numbers and allegedly too 'lazy' to work long hours on plantations) to develop sugar and other export crops that were to make Hawaii an

Before meshing of beaches was introduced shark attacks were frequent in Sydney and the only defensive action was to send out the surf boat and try to spear the monsters.

The shark has been described as the perfect killing machine, and this 15 foot 1,300 pounder fits that description. It was caught in Northern California waters.

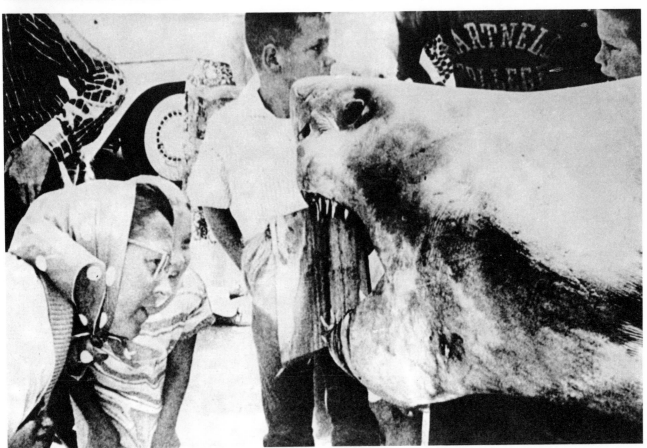

In the first years of meshing, hundreds of sharks were caught off the New South Wales beaches—including this monster.

economic appendage to the United States. In the 1890s—with their ancient culture in ruins, their population dwindled to a fraction of its former strength, and much of their land in foreign hands—the Hawaiians experienced the final shattering blow when the settlers deposed Queen Lili'uokalani and successfully negotiated the annexation of Hawaii to the United States. During this traumatic century and a quarter it is surprising that any feature of pre-European Hawaiian life could survive, particularly if it was an activity like surfing that rankled the missionaries so. Why the powerful missionaries were dead-set against surfing is not difficult to surmise: they were strict Calvinists to whom carefree enjoyment—particularly if it involved, as did surfing, sex, gambling, and

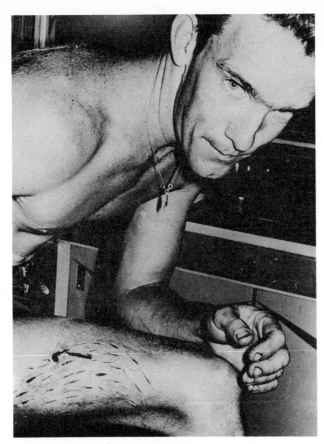

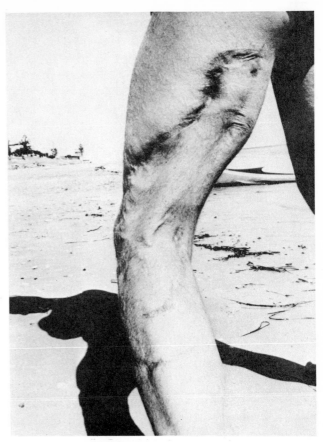

Roy McCuffie, a machinist from Cairns in North Queensland, was one of the few victims of the shark to survive. He was seized by a shark on a beach near Cairns, but the shark let go. On his thigh are thirty teeth marks, up to ¼ inch deep.

The wounds the shark makes are frightful in their extent. This Australian bears the scars from an attack by a white pointer. He was lucky to keep his leg and his life.

An item of Surf Life Saving equipment developed in Australia is the surf boat, used to chase away sharks and for rescues beyond the reach of a lifeline.

The Australian surf boat is an integral part of surf carnivals.

Surf Carnivals

neglect of domestic and religious duties— was abhorrent. While their English colleague William Ellis could describe Hawaiian surfing with admiration, many of these American missionaries were bitter in their opposition to it. Their righteous attitude towards surfing is clearly revealed in the following denunciation of it and other 'rough' Hawaiian sports: 'The evils resulting from all these sports and amusements have in part been named. Some lost their lives thereby, some were severely wounded, maimed and crippled; some were reduced to poverty, both by losses in gambling and by neglecting to cultivate the land; and the instances were not a few in which they were reduced to utter starvation. But the greatest evil of all resulted from the constant intermingling, without any restraint, of persons

Surf boat race start at a carnival at
Warriewood beach near Sydney.

Going out on a practice run.

Going out in the surf boat can be hazardous and always quite spectacular.

Even in the smaller surfs the boat crews take a hammering.

of both sexes and of all ages, at all times of the day and at all hours of the night . . . . '
Almost from the moment they set foot on Hawaii the missionaries began urging the Hawaiians to give up surfing and other amusements distasteful to their puritan eyes. In 1826, for example, a missionary influenced the chiefs of Oahu to send an edict through the streets of Honolulu exhorting the people to give up their games and turn to the Christian teaching. This missionary attitude brought bitter criticism from some non-missionary foreigners, and in 1838, a visitor maintained that: 'A change has taken place in certain customs . . . . I allude to the variety of athletic exercises such as swimming, with or without a surfboard, dancing, wrestling, throwing the javelin, etc., all of which games, being in opposition to the strict tenets of Calvinism, have been suppressed . . . . Can the missionaries be charged with suppressing these games? I believe they deny having done so. But they write and publicly express their opinions, and state these sports to be expressly against the laws of God, and by a succession of reasoning,

which may be readily traced, impress upon the minds of the chiefs and others, the idea that all who practise them, secure themselves the displeasure of offended heaven. Then the chiefs, from a spontaneous benevolence, at once interrupt customs so hazardous to their vassals.' At least one missionary, the formidable Hiram Bingham, vigorously rejected this charge and declared the missionaries to be innocent of suppressing Hawaiian pastimes. He wrote, for example, that: 'The decline and discontinuance of the use of the surfboard, as civilization advances, may be accounted for by the increase in modesty, industry and religion, without supposing, as some have affected to believe, that missionaries caused oppressive enactments against it.' To Bingham the Christianized Hawaiian had become too modest to appear dressed in only a loincloth—or less—in the surf, and was too busy working and attending to his religious duties to have time for leisurely activities. In effect, then, while claiming

And it gets worse . . .

. . . and worse. Note the stroke in this boat has fallen flat on his back.

This crew is going to carry an awful lot of water out to the buoys and back.

that missionary rules did not prohibit surfing, Bingham was admitting that the Christianization of the Hawaiians had indeed contributed to the decline of surfing.

The Hawaiians of the time should not, however, be thought of as passive automatons controlled by the missionaries. Many Hawaiians were excited by the new skills missionaries offered to teach them, particularly reading and writing which they saw as one of the keys of the foreigners' obvious power and technological superiority. They therefore abandoned themselves to the task of learning to read and write in numerous missionary schools hastily erected around the countryside. And, in at least one instance, their enthusiasm for the new learning led them to take their once treasured surfboards and saw them up to make seats and writing tables for a new schoolhouse on Kauai. However much weight one assigns to any

Through into the calm sea ahead.

Through the shorebreak and now it's flat out to the buoys.

100

But this one is not going much further.

This crew hasn't made it, the next step is for the boat to broach and crew, oars and boat will be in a turmoil in the water.

But if the going out is full of peril . . .

. . . the coming back can be equally terrifying. This boat has lost its sweep man and they'll not get very far without him . . .

individual factor, there can be no doubt that all of them together—population loss, social, economic and political upheavals, missionary pressures and Hawaiian enthusiasm for new activities—contributed to the decline of Hawaii's once favourite pastime. But, it is obvious that surfing did not die out completely as did most Hawaiian games and sports like *kōnane* checkers, *hōlua* sledding or *'ulu maika* bowling. Emerson's mourning over surfing's demise and the disappearance of the surfboard from Hawaii's beaches was premature, for there was still a little life left in the sport when the Hawaiians entered the 20th century.

. . . they've made it. They are on a wave and the crew scrambles to the back of the boat to keep the nose up.

This crew didn't make it. The wave has curled under the boat and it has gone into a nose dive.

Like the Vikings of old, and just as spectacular.

Coming in on a wave with good control—weight at the back, nose up, screaming for the shore.

These two crews, from Newport and Freshwater beaches near Sydney, have collided in the break. They are out of the race, now to clean up the mess.

By the turn of the century surfing was a rare sight along the coasts of the 'outer islands'— Niihau, Kauai, Molokai, Maui, Lanai and Hawaii—and the only significant focus of surfing seems to have been around Waikiki Beach, then on the outskirts of Honolulu, the chief port city and capital of the new Territory of Hawaii. If surfing was to survive anywhere in Hawaii, it is not surprising that the Waikiki area of Oahu was its last bastion for by 1900 about one-quarter of the few Hawaiians who survived were living in or around this area.

Waikiki surfing at this time was, however, but a relic of the once proud sport. Only a handful

Home for a win on a calm day, when it was rowing all the way.

Fighting for first place, two boats collide and are out of the race.

Marathon surf boat races are also part of the surf scene, with crews rowing up to 30 miles. Here the Coledale boat makes it home first in the Captain Cook Marathon surf boat race. The crew was near to exhaustion.

Freshwater crew bail out and start bailing out. They've been swamped on a wave.

of surfers might be seen surfing together in the many breaks at Waikiki, and conspicuously absent from the waves were the chiefly champions who once dominated the sport. The surfing temples were in ruins, and the great sports festivals of the *Makahiki* celebrations and other sacred aspects of the sport had been largely if not totally forgotten. Few, if any, women surfed. And, surfing contests with lively betting among surfers and spectators were a thing of the past. To anyone acquainted with the glories of ancient Hawaiian surfing, Waikiki surfing in the first years of this century must have seemed a tame pastime indeed.

By this time the expert boardmakers of old had died out, and what boards were being made were crude copies of the finely shaped boards of a hundred years previous. The

A Sydney surf power boat on patrol. Fast to reach swimmers in danger, the power boats nevertheless will not entirely replace the spectacular man-powered surf boats which are part of the Australian beach tradition.

The power surf boats are expensive and generally beyond the reach of surf club finances, so business and charity organizations come to the 'rescue'.

The modern surf boat is being introduced onto Australian beaches. Jet boats, they can run up onto the sand and are easily pushed into the water.

Fleet of powered surf boats on display during a Sydney beach carnival.

manufacture of *olo* boards seems to have ceased altogether, and most, if not all, boards made were short, thick planks—usually hewn from redwood or other imported woods—that bore only a superficial resemblance to their closest ancient counterpart, the thin, sleek *alaia* board. These 'new' boards seem to have been mainly in the six- to eight-foot range, to be wide and to have thick, shapeless siderails. As might be expected from the relative crudity of design, their performance was probably no match for the *alaia* boards of old. The ancient technique of sliding across a wave at an angle seems to have been lost or rare; most descriptions of the sport from this period depict the surfers riding straight in on the break with a minimum of manoeuvring.

For example, the picture of Waikiki surfing in 1907 presented by Charmian London, the wife of the famous American writer Jack London, shows how tame the art of surfing had become: 'The thick board, somewhat coffin-shaped, with rounded ends, should be over six

Duke Kahanamoku

No single man had a greater influence on surfing throughout its history than Hawaiian, Duke Kahanamoku. In 1918, still just a boy, he had proven himself to be the fastest swimmer in the world six years before at the 1912 Olympic Games.

feet long for adults. This plank is floated out to the breaking water, which can be done either wading alongside or lying face-downward paddling, and there you wait for the right wave. When you see it coming, stand ready to launch the board on the gathering slope, spring upon it, and—keep on going if you can. Lie flat on your chest, hands grasping the sides of the large end of the heavy timber, and steer with your feet. The expert, having gauged the right speed, rises cautiously to his knees, to full stature, and then, erect with feet in the churning foam, makes straight for the beach . . . '

Kahanamoku surfing at Waikiki in 1915, the year he brought the surfboard out of Hawaii and to Australia. The Duke, with partner, riding tandem.

By the early 1900s it was evident that surfing had retrogressed several hundred if not a thousand years, and was probably not much more highly evolved than it was when the first Polynesian settlers in Hawaii began to develop the true surfboard and to perfect surfing techniques. Practised only by a few people who

111

used rudimentary boards with unspectacular skill, and stripped of the cultural features that had once made it a great sport rather than a simple recreation, surfing may be said to have returned to its infancy.

At this point surfing's decline might have continued but for new demographic and social conditions. Population decrease among the Hawaiians was being arrested, and direct rule from the United States brought new political and economic stability to the islands. The tie between Hawaii and the United States also brought new people to Hawaii, people of an entirely different character from many of the

The Duke in Australia. In this picture taken at Freshwater Beach the Duke has Fred Williams beside him, wearing a moustache, and beside him again is Australian Olympic swimmer, Harry Hay.

Americans who formerly dominated the islands, and this new population element was to have a profound effect on surfing's future. The *Haoles*, as the Hawaiians called the Americans and other people of northern European ancestry, who settled in Hawaii during the 19th century, had been for the most part hopelessly lost when it came to surfing. The puritanical missionaries had not dared to try this 'devil's pastime', nor had many other *Haole* settlers and visitors ventured into the surf. One visitor who did, the popular American humourist Mark Twain who travelled around Hawaii in the 1860s, chronicled his floundering

The Duke remained intensely involved in surfing all his life.

The Duke and some friends home in Hawaii in 1920.

attempts to ride the waves and declared categorically that: 'None but natives ever master the art of surf-bathing thoroughly.' *Haole* clumsiness in the water, and fear of the surf, was even rationalized in the popular belief that only an Hawaiian could ever hope to learn how to stand and balance on a surfboard. However, the new settlers who came to Hawaii after annexation, and even some of the island-born sons of long-time settlers, had different ideas. By this time Americans had developed a passion for swimming and bathing in the sea, and this new breed of *Haoles* was not going to let the opportunity to learn how to surf go to waste. So by watching Hawaiian surfers and

The Duke in his middle age poses on Waikiki with his redwood koa surfboard.

He had a style and swiftness in the water that was amazing.

Still surfing at 60, and still showing plenty of style.

114

following their instructions a few of them began to learn to master a surfboard. The schoolboys of Honolulu were at the forefront of this *Haole* surfing movement. They started spending their afternoons and weekends at Waikiki riding the waves, and more than one of them would skip classes during the week if the waves were running high.

Just as this surfing movement was getting underway the development of Waikiki as a resort area threatened to pinch it off. The new and eager surfers, who stored their boards and changed their clothes in the bushes along the unoccupied shore, found their hideaways being cleared away for the construction of new

The Duke with his wife, Nadine.

Surfing still, the Duke, aged 77. This picture was taken in August, 1967, just five months before his death.

After the Duke's visit to Australia surfing took off. Australians soon became expert. Here surfing personality, 'Snow' McAlister, performs his characteristic surfing head stand.

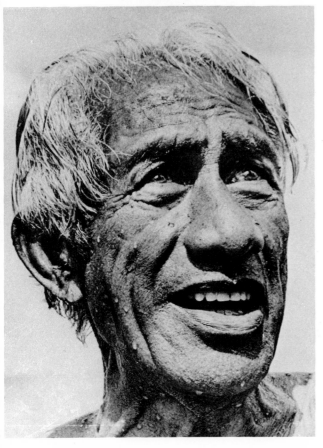

115

residences and hotels, and that the proprietors of these beachfront properties wanted to bar their access to the beach. Fortunately, at this point a group of newly-arrived American businessmen had a different vision of how Waikiki should be developed. They recognized the uniqueness of surfing and believed that it should be promoted both as a healthy sport for Hawaii's youth, and as an attraction to draw tourists to the islands. Under the leadership of Alexander Ford, and with the aid of publicity provided by Jack London who published an article on the 'royal sport' in an American national magazine, this group started a campaign to keep the beach open to surfers and to boost the sport's growth.

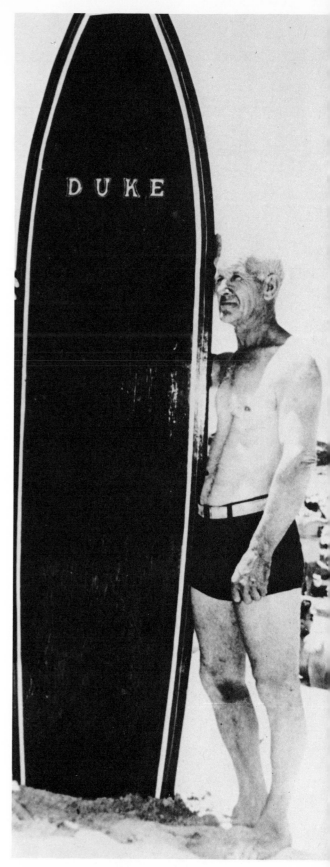

One of the youngsters impressed by Duke Kahanamoku on his Australian visit was Claude West. West became Australian champion and held that title for many years afterwards. He is shown here, years after his retirement from active surfing, with the board the Duke made on his Australian visit and presented to West on his departure.

An Australian surfing legend, Justin 'Snow' McAlister, who became surfboard champion of Australia in 1924 and held that title until 1927.

Still surfing. 'Snow' McAlister with his surf ski and Mick Dooley, fifth in the World Board-Riding Championships of 1964. McAlister and Dooley had just ridden the bombora at Long Reef near Sydney when this picture was taken.

The surfboard grew slowly in popularity through the 1920s and 1930s, but they were different boards to those in use today. These are club members at Manly near Sydney.

McAlister remained an active surfer all his life. He is pictured here on Manly Beach with a surf ski, an Australian invention, with which McAlister was very adept.

Champions of the Thirties

The Australian Surfboard Champions of the 1930s, left to right, Geoff Cohen, Harry Wicke, Jimmy Austin and Lou Morath.

The style in vogue on the old hollow boards was a fairly simple one.

In 1908 these promoters founded the Hawaiian Outrigger Canoe Club for the express purpose of 'preserving surfing on boards and in Hawaiian outrigger canoes,' and leased beachfront property from the estate of the late Queen Emma to give surfers an assured access to the beach and the waves beyond. There they built grass huts for changing clothes and storing boards, thus giving surfers a 'home' on the beach. With the opening of these new facilities interest in the sport increased dramatically, and the number of surfers multiplied rapidly. Surfing contests and exhibitions were held at Waikiki that gained national publicity in the United States, and within a few years surfing was indeed established as a top tourist attraction in Hawaii. By 1911 the sport had become so popular among Honolulu residents and visitors to Waikiki that as many as a hundred surfers—not the 'handful' of a few years previous—could be seen surfing at Waikiki on weekends.

The rider did little more than stand erect . . . and head into the shore.

In those early days even a few women tried their arm.

As surfing's popularity grew, lost skills were regained, and boards grew in length and improved in design and craftsmanship. The new generation of surfers, equipped with sleek boards of ten feet or more in length, re-discovered the ancient technique of *lala* and were soon sliding across the waves with ease instead of surfing straight in. In 1915 Jack London returned to Hawaii to find that the Outrigger Canoe Club had some twelve hundred members, modern facilities, and what seemed '. . . like a half a mile of surf-board lockers'. During this trip London's wife once again wrote about surfing, and her account shows how much progress had been made since her first visit eight years previous: 'The newest brood of surf-boarders had learned and put into practice angles never dreamed of a decade earlier. Now, instead of always coasting at right-angles to the wave, young Lorrin P. Thurston and the half-dozen who shared with him the reputation of being the most skilled, would often be seen erect on boards that their feet and balance guided at astonishing slants.' While *Haoles* had played a crucial role in reviving surfing, and the Outrigger Canoe Club was basically a *Haole* organization, Hawaiian interest and expertise grew along with that of the *Haoles*. The Hawaiians formed their own surfing club, the *Hui Nalu* (literally, 'Wave Club'), and two of the Waikiki champions of the day were Hawaiians: George Freeth and Duke Kahanamoku. Both literally grew up in the water at Waikiki, developed into top surfers there and then went overseas to be the first to spread surfing beyond Hawaii's shores.

George Freeth was Hawaii's first surfing ambassador. In 1907, when he was the reigning champion at Waikiki, Freeth was hired by the Pacific Electric railroad company to introduce surfing to the Los Angeles public which the company hoped to lure into making regular trips to the seashore in its railway carriages. At Redondo Beach, and at other beaches along the Southern California coast, Freeth gave surfing demonstrations and lessons to spark interest in the sport among young Californians. Five years later Duke Kahanamoku travelled

Board man Harry Wicke, Australian champion, 1939, 1940.

The types of boards in vogue in Australia in the late 1930s and early 40s. The board third from the left is a surf ski.

through Southern California to the 1912 Olympic Games where he proved himself to be the world's fastest swimmer. Kahanamoku was also a top surfer, and stopped in California long enough to astound crowds with his surfing skill at several beaches along the coast. Kahanamoku belonged to the new generation of surfers developing then at Waikiki and was thus able to show Californians, who had learned the rudiments of surfing from Freeth, all the new techniques. Kahanamoku's brief visit built up a tremendous enthusiasm for the sport, and

Fred Notting, New South Wales Surfboard Champion 1944, 1945.

Meanwhile, back in Hawaii, the Hawaiians were doing what their ancestors had been practising for centuries.

Another significant influence on the international surfing scene was the American, Tom Blake, here driving to the shore at Palos Verdes, California, about 1937.

Up and down the Californian coast the surfboard became increasingly popular. This was the scene on Palos Verdes in the summer of 1939.

soon Californians were building surfboards and teaching themselves how to surf all up and down the southern coast of the state. With many beaches and headlands open to ocean swells that swept in, according to the season, from either north or south Pacific storm centres, and a growing tradition of outdoor living among its residents, California was a 'natural' for the first successful transplant of Hawaiian surfing.

While surfing was being revived in Hawaii and transplanted to California, in Australia another and distinctly different surfing movement was coming to life. And what an extraordinary birth it was, following a

124

Tom Blake, surfboard designer, with some of his early models.

One of the first of the surfboard clubs in the United States—The Palos Verdes Surfing Club. Front row, Gene Hornbeck, Patty Townsend, Kay Murray; back row, E. Lenkeit, Jim Reynolds, Doc. Ball, E. J. O'Shier, and C. Clark.

Doc. Ball on his 14-foot paddle board at Hermosa Pier.

pregnancy that was more than a century long. It was while Captain Cook was on his voyages of discovery that put Australia on the map that his monarch, George III made sea bathing fashionable in England. Certainly up until that time bathing, even in the privacy of a household tub, was distinctly unpopular and in many sections of society, even unknown. The question of immersing oneself in the sea voluntarily was unthinkable. But George III's medical advisers suggested his health might improve if he bathed daily in the salt waters of the English Channel. The King took the advice and immediately all the fashionable doctors began ordering the same treatment for their fashionable patients, and the ladies and gentlemen of quality took to the seas in droves as they had formerly taken to the spa resorts. The puritan streak in the Anglo-Saxon was not so evident in those days as it was to become under Queen Victoria later. There were no neck-to-knee costumes involved in the social splashes of the 1770s. According to the *London Bystander* of the time '... Majesty himself, Majesty's sons and daughters, the most noble Lords and ladies, the most respected of the landed gentry and their better halves bathed in the sea as Aphrodite might have done, or Adam and Eve before the apple. Naturally, the women

Hermosa Pier in 1940.

Soon everybody was doing it—Palos Verdes Cove in 1937.

126

From the late 1930s board-riding was confined to orthodox styles.

bathed in one spot and the men in the other, and as remotely as possible—a custom that obtained even after costumes of the most voluminous design were made compulsory.' Victorian prudery knocked on the head any prospect of George III's sea-bathing habits developing into the international cult surfing is today. Outside of Hawaii and parts of the California coast the beaches of the world were deserted, rather alien places where only the occasional paddler could be seen rinsing his or her ankles or, in a few of the more populated centres, taking the waters via the bathing machine. These were the macabre invention of

In 1939 Australia sent overseas its first surf team—to the Pacific Games in Honolulu. Photo shows Australian team member, surfboard rider Lou Morath, left, and right on a training spin.

127

The Surf Ski

The heavy boards that were in vogue before the Malibu lacked manoeuvreability so the riders looked to other directions for diversion. Tom Blake with his dog Rusty.

Englishman Benjamin Beale in 1780 and were used in Britain and in Australia right up to and into the 20th century, when the bathing machine was considered to be the only way in which people could respectably approach the sea. They stood in rows back from the sea front looking rather like large gypsy caravans. The would-be bather entered the cabin of the machine fully clothed and while he or she was undressing an old horse would be coupled on by an attendant and the box was towed into the sea. On the seaward side, huge hoods formed a funnel so that the bather could enter the water unseen. A couple of dunks in the water, the bather re-entered the machine and it was towed back to dry land, with much bumping and jerking about.

Surfing might have stayed right there, locked in all those inhibitions, for perhaps another half century or more had it not been for the developing character of the Australian. The polyglot community of convicts, remittance men and free settlers from the Old World who

Boards, surf skis and surf boats together at Manly Beach in the 1930s.

The water was there to be exploited. Not only the board was coming into tourist use, but also the Hawaiian canoes.

A Tahitian canoe.

The Tahitians could also see the potential of their ancient water sports for modern tourists.

had made up the first Australian community following Captain Cook's discovery of the country, had, a century later, shaken itself into some sort of shape. Life in a hard and hostile country had given the Australian of the 1880s three major characteristics—an independence of spirit, a contempt for authority and a hard, strong body which he liked to exercise. When those characteristics were placed side by side with the 12,000 miles of coastline ringing Australia, almost all of it in the form of

The European surfer made his version of the Hawaiian canoe, this one at Coogee Beach, Sydney.

Competitor in Surf Carnival at Bondi, Sydney.

The surf ski was an Australian invention of the early 1930s, which quickly became popular and is today still part of the equipment of Australian Surf Life Saving Clubs.

golden beaches, it was only a matter of time before the Australian defied authority and took the plunge. The authority was, in the light of more modern thinking, incredible. For a start it was forbidden by law to 'bathe in waters exposed to view from any wharf, street, public place or dwelling house between the hours of 6 a.m. and 8 p.m.'. Any Australian who wanted to use his magnificent beaches had to do so early in the morning or late at night. But there were those who chafed under such

Riding with a surf ski to shore.

Coming in on a comber at Bondi this surf skier gets into a little tangle with his paddle.

A team of lifesavers with their surf skis at Manly in 1937.

authority and one of them was Albert G. Hanson, of the Sydney suburb of Concord who was perhaps the first Australian to brave the surf when in 1876 he and his three children, along with George Thornton, one-time Mayor of the City of Sydney, went to Manly and entered the surf in webbing bathing trunks. Soon after this Hanson went to England, but on his return in 1885 he went back to Manly and began bathing again. Other men watched his enjoyment and followed him into the water

Beach belle with her surf ski at Manly in 1941.

The usual week-end scene at Manly Beach —surf skis, long boards, malibus and riders.

which gave rise to a rash of protests being made to the Manly Council about the habits of men bathing on the municipality's beaches 'in a state of semi-nudity'. The council called in the police who caught up with Hanson and told him they had instructions to prosecute anyone caught bathing between 6 a.m. and 8 p.m. Hanson had to change his habits and take to swimming between 5 a.m. and 6 a.m. but the battle was on—a battle that lasted another fifty years before the Australians who wanted to

Riding with surf ski on the shore breaks.

The youngsters took up the surf skis, too, and couldn't resist the urge to try and stand.

Surf skiers in the early morning taking
advantage of a good surf.

enjoy the freedom of the world's best beaches
finally defeated the puritans and the prudes,
the politicians, the council authorities and the
police.

For one would-be surfer, the fight was
frustratingly easy. He was William Gocher, a
short, thinly built man of middle age who
edited the small local newspaper in Manly.
In 1902, tired of seeing his readers suffering the
indignities of creeping to the beaches before
dawn and creeping home again at first light, he
announced in his columns that he would bathe
at mid-day on the next Sunday, from Manly's
ocean beach. He carried out the threat and no
action followed from either the Manly Council
or the police. So he repeated the process the
next Sunday after announcing it again in his
newspaper, and again on a third Sunday. Again
no police action, no threat of arrest, so an
angry Gocher went to the then Police
Commissioner in Sydney and asked him to

A surf ski race was a regular event at Sydney Surf Carnivals.

Paul Kibble and Arthur Salaris of
Swansea-Belmont winning the double surf
ski event at a Warriewood, N.S.W. carnival.

clarify the situation. Gocher was told the police intended taking no action against daylight bathers, as long as they were suitably dressed. Gocher reported this in his newspaper and the rush to the surf was on.

Authority had far from given up the fight, however. Police patrolled other Sydney beaches taking the names of this daylight bather and that and prosecutions followed, those convicted being fined two pounds for their 'indecency'. The farcical situation came to something of a head when one man, whose name was taken for swimming at Bondi, turned out to be the Rector of the Waverley Church of St. Mary's . He was brought before the courts and admonished, but the wave of criticism that followed put a stop to the name-taking by police and the local councils shifted their ground. They listened to the prudes amongst their voters and ratepayers and decided to draft their own regulations governing the attire of

Australian lifesavers on double surf skis smash their way through the breakers at the start of a Coogee Surf Carnival race.

The veteran 'Snow' McAlister rides a surf ski at Manly in 1962.

Other methods of shooting the breakers were always cropping up. In the 1930s rubber surf floats became the vogue on beaches all over the world.

the public using their beaches. The Mayors of the suburbs of Manly, Randwick and Waverley, covering the main Sydney beaches, met together and were there told by Mayor Watkins of Waverley that 'some of these surfbathers are nothing but exhibitionists, putting on V trunks and exposing themselves twisted into all shapes in the sand. They are in worse manner than if they were nude. Their garments after contact with the water show up the figure too prominently. Women are often worse than

There was no end to invention in the early days of the surf. This was an attempt at putting a motor onto a solid long board as a 'surf scooter'.

Surfing Inventions

Visiting English boys after trying out rubber floats in the surf on a visit to Australia.

The Australian inventor tried out his motor surf scooter at Bondi. Its popularity was about as great as its floatation.

men, putting on light, gauzy material that clings when wet too much to be decent. But they won't continue doing it at Bondi Beach, not as long as I am Mayor Watkins.'

So the Mayors between them decided that any person over the age of four years swimming in their baths and on their beaches had to be 'decently clad'—in a cumbersome woollen suit of long knickerbockers reaching half way down the calf, covered by a thick jumper with half sleeves, the bottom of the jumper covering to

There was no age limit on the enjoyment of the surf, and when light plastic foam boards could be made cheaply for the youngsters, a whole new world opened to them.

Surf riders come in all styles . . .

. . . riding a board and hula hooping on the way in. These experts at Huntington Beach, California.

just below the buttocks, the top tight around the neck. If you didn't wear that garish outfit, you were thrown off the beach and stood the risk of being fined up to £10, a considerable sum in those days.

The police were on hand to enforce the regulations on the beaches and some strange persecutions were the lot of the keen Australian embryo surfer. One of them recalled, half a century later: 'We were forced to leave the Manly beach because the police were at us all

In Japan, artificial waves can be made if the real ones aren't available. In a swimming pool of a recreation centre in Tokyo, two foot high artificially made waves give enthusiasts a good ride.

Skim boards enjoyed a vogue also. A thin sheet of plywood was flung flat onto very shallow water and the rider jumped aboard to get a long, skidding ride.

the time to see that our costumes were proper. The sun was a great temptation to bare the skin to it, but the police wouldn't have it. We left Manly and took to riding the horse tram down to the far northern end of the cove at Queenscliff and then taking shank's pony across the sandhills to the next beach at Freshwater. But here we again became subject to regulations, policemen stalking us while we lay in the sand dunes and baked. It was always necessary to keep a sharp lookout for police,

Even body surfing went through its variations. Here an enthusiast 'Shoots the Breakers'—from behind a speedboat!

Hanging ten behind a speedboat on the Tweed River in northern New South Wales.

but I have never been able to ascertain their reason for hunting us in such an out of the way place as Freshwater, with only about three or four houses in all of the area, considering that our costumes were never rolled down below the waistline.'

All of this was bringing the police and the councils into ridicule and not affecting the popularity of the new recreation of surfbathing one bit. From the handful of brave men who dared to go in at Manly early in the morning,

within a few years Bondi Beach was aswarm
with 30,000 on any hot Sunday, and by that
time the girls had followed the boys in,
accepting their assurance that 'the water's fine'.
But while the police gradually withdrew from
their beach patrol activities, the puritan
pressure on the local councils continued and
the Manly Council issued a new regulation
insisting that all women bathers wore a full
skirt over their neck to knee costume—a
regulation made without any thought being

Wayne Burton, short of waves, attached
his surfboard to a speed boat for a new
style of water skiing.

given to the cumbersome nature of such a dress in the boisterous Manly surf, or the dangers of undertows.

The councils retreated slowly, being harassed behind the while by the puritans, and later ordinances left the question of dress on the beaches to the will of the bather, provided the garb satisfied the local police as to its propriety. By then the bathers themselves had decided upon their own rules—largely set by the fashions reaching them from the bathing world

Body surfing became tremendously popular with Australians after its introduction at the turn of the century by a young Polynesian.

Body Surfing

Any day when the surf's up on Australian beaches, the young men—and occasionally a few girls—are out in the deep water waiting for a wave that will take them to shore.

Taking off to ride a wave to shore on a Sydney beach.

Heading for shore. The surfer keeps feet up to keep his body inclination forward so that the wave will carry him along.

overseas—and the men wore a full costume from the neck to half way down the thighs, with a pair of V-trunks pulled over them. The women went for the 'Canadian costume' of mid-thigh knickerbockers and a tunic with short sleeves, a rounded neck and of a length reaching to just below the buttocks. However that sounds today, the costume must have had some charm in those early days, for a contemporary writer then had this to say: 'The Canadian costume, when made of wool,

A good ride—arms tucked into the body—heading for shore at a rate of knots.

Caught in a dumping wave, the surfer brings hands forward to balance his body up in the air and avoid a wipe out.

seems to be specially designed by providence to meet the requirements of feminine bathers. The average girl when she commences surfbathing, shrinks from notice, and chooses a costume of amplitude. After a few weeks of experience she no longer shrinks, but the costume does; and, as she gradually grows indifferent to public gaze, the Canadian costume gradually assumes proportions at once useful and picturesque, but proportions which, when she started bathing, she would have regarded as woefully inadequate.'

The debate and controversy over the dress of the surfbathers was to go on in Australia for many more years, but surfing had come to stay. By 1910 there were so many surfbathers on the Australian beaches, a writer of the day, Edgar T. Russell, was able to report in *The Lone Hand* magazine that surfbathing had 'become an institution as important to Australia as standing armies, established

Ready for a wipe out—the surfer was too low in the wave, which will tip his legs over in front of him and send him to the bottom.

A really big wave for one surfer.

Perfectly positioned on the wave, a surfer would be thrust forward in the break and, with luck, get a run all the way to shore.

Sheer delight. A body surfer, Geoff Love, takes a big one across the face at Shark Island, Cronulla, N.S.W.

Australians begin body surfing and become expert at it before their teens. Here a couple of young masters show how it's done.

churches, music halls and sturdy beggars are in older civilizations'. Indeed, in a few short years surfing became a cult in Australia that was to produce a hardening of the national character and changes and innovations in countries all over the world blessed with sea coasts. A degree of tolerance was accorded the sea bathers, they were no longer regarded as cranks, or brazen, or lewd. Articles began appearing in the press describing the geographic and hydrostatic requirements of the best surfing

Heading for shore, a body surfer well placed on the top of the wave for the run downhill to the beach.

beaches where good waves would be produced, there were other stories boosting the health-giving properties of seawater in commotion as it crashed on the yellow sands. Ratepayers in the seaside council areas ceased their bleatings as property values soared. For instance, in the five years that followed William Gocher's publicized gesture of bathing in view at mid-day on Sundays, Manly's population increased by fifty per cent; house rents and rates doubled; property values increased by from 50 to

An 8-foot wave can look like approaching doom to the surfer at its foot.

While a board rider prepares to paddle over the top of the wave a body surfer shoots through the curl flying across the break.

The body surfer heads for a wipe out.

Women can master the art of body surfing, too. This girl is using a small paddle board strapped to her wrist allowing her to cut across the face of the wave.

300 per cent. Suddenly the beaches were such a colourful, virile scene, everyone had to be near them, everyone wanted to live by them, be part of them. The exercise in the foam, the browning effects of the sun, the magnificent freedom of it all resulted very quickly in the situation where on any Sydney beach on a Saturday or Sunday you would find a collection of strapping athletes the like and numbers of which could not be found anywhere else in the world.

The surfing beaches became the society of the time. Not only because everybody was doing it, but because all the ingredients were there that fitted the developing Australian character, the natural follow-on to the convict settlement start to the colony a century before —the classless society. Under the sun, in the boiling surf, in the standard costume decreed by the local councils, recognizing no barriers or distinctions, everyone was the same. Unless, that is, one was a 'newcomer'. The newcomers

An Australian body surfer in action, using flippers, to get extra momentum in the take-off in a big surf.

The kind of wave one avoids in body surfing. A 'dumper', it breaks suddenly and violently, dropping the surfer straight down to the bottom.

were easy to spot, they were white, while everyone else was burnt by the sun to a rich brown. Indeed white looked so bad, browning was considered to be a requirement of both God and nature and out of this the easy-going, don't worry about tomorrow cult of the sun-lover that is inherent in the Australian character today, had its beginnings. But the democracy of the beach was the most significant product of those early days. The lady in her carriage through the week, looking

Styles of Riding Machines

The first board riders outside California to try out the Malibu took it easily.

With a flipper to get momentum, a belly board—a very short version of the Malibu—proves highly manoeuvreable in good surfs.

splendid, lost out heavily to the little laundry girl next door when both were side by side in their swimsuits at the beach on Sunday. The alleged 'near nakedness' of the Sydney beaches in those days was a great social leveller, and as one writer of the time pointed out: 'The social distinctions of the beaches are something so old as to seem new. They are the social distinctions which prevailed in the days before history was written, and when man was still able to hold on tight with his big toe. The

The more manoeuvreable the boards became the more variations were tried out. Here crack United States surfer, Hobie Alter, and his wife do some tandem riding at Florida Gardens.

Speeding for shore on a belly board, John Arnold on the beaches of South Australia.

A sight not often seen, body surfer and belly board rider on the same wave. The beaches of the world have become so crowded, board riders and body surfers are today in separate areas.

There's a crash coming. Two winter surfers get their lines crossed.

lifesavers represent the very highest class. They are the Samurais, the oligarchs, the elite. They strut the beaches with superiority that is insolent, yet, at the same time, tolerant of the short comings of lesser breeds—a gladiator class, envied by all the men, adored by all the women. The rest of the little cosmos of the beach is divided by class distinctions as rigid as those of ante-revolutionary France. The shooter represents the aristocracy but, if he cannot shoot, a bather may at least rise to full heights of citizenship by lying in the sun until he acquires the necessary brown tint. The white man represents the pariah class, despised by all; and if he would survive it is for him to adopt nature's protective provision of taking on the colour of his surroundings as soon as possible. The regular bather may endure the white legs of a girl bather if they are otherwise very nice; but the man, be he as mighty as

Winter surfing calls for a wet suit to keep out the cold, but the rewards are there in bigger, better waves.

First the novice lies on his board, then graduates to his knees.

155

Hackenschmidt himself, will be treated with contumely and scorn if he omits within reasonable time to put on the coat of tan that bespeaks experience.'

The social pattern set, the social rules followed. The writer of the above referred to two phenomena that were Australian developments which were to travel around the world just as the Hawaiian sport of kings—surf riding—spread across the world. Lifesaving as it developed in Australia became an institution

Screaming across the face of the wave on a belly board makes for exhilarating riding.

unique to man and was adopted by scores of countries. Surf shooting was a development of the ancient Pacific sport of shooting waves not with a board, but with a body, and it can be truly said that the Australians today are more expert in this art than are the Hawaiians themselves, or any other nationality, for that matter.

Surf shooting in Australia began, as so many things in surf began, at the Sydney suburb of Manly, just before the turn of the century.

A youngster gets the feel of the sport on a lightweight foam plastic board.

Novice board rider and body surfer going for the same wave.

The youngsters get their training in various ways. Here a nine-year-old tries out his style on a rubber float.

The wipe-outs occur just the same.

An ungraceful ending.

Having become experts of the board themselves, Australians introduced board-riding into the cold surfs of Britain.

Surfing in Britain

Surfbathing had been just that—men and women, just a few of the latter, went down to the sea and did little more than paddle, or stand up to their waists in the foam and splash about. The Hawaiian sport, whether on boards or with the body, was unknown. But at this time there was in Manly village a teenage Polynesian boy named Tommy Tanna, who had come to Australia on a trading ship and stayed to work as a gardener's boy in Manly. At every chance he got he was down at Manly, in the surf, giving himself reminders of his home. He was no ankle dipper or up-to-the-waist splasher. He swam out past the astonished few on the edge who felt certain this dark-skinned lad was either a dervish or bent on suicide. He swam on through the tumult of the breaking waves, diving under the break to emerge still swimming, on the other side. When he reached the line where the seas were mounting up ready to tip forward into a wave of boiling foam, he swam with

Along the Cornish coast in Britain good waves were found by the nomadic board riders.

All rugged up on the shore, freezing in the water, the British surfer has to be hardy in the extreme.

one or two strokes onto the wave and let it propel him at speed, in to the shore, only his head and shoulders emerging from the front of the wave. Of course, it caused a sensation amongst the onlookers, one of whom happened to be a seventeen-year-old Australian boy called Freddie Williams. This, he had to do, and do it he did after a lot of practice, discovering just which wave to pick, when to start swimming before it so as to be caught up in its rush forward and carried along with it,

160

The British surfer, despite his climate, is cast in the same mould as surfers everywhere.

Surfing in Britain is not always comfortable.

rather than being pushed under to bob up after the tumult has passed, half drowned. He made friends with Tanna, but Tanna was no teacher, he was a doer. He demonstrated to Williams how he held his body, his hands to his side, shoulders hunched, his head lowered, his trunk and legs inclined upwards so that the weight of the wave pushed him forward, how he kicked with his legs to keep up momentum and remain steady in the wave. Williams practised and practised and mastered

161

the trick to the point where he was not only better than Tanna, but was regarded as the greatest exponent of the sport the country had seen, even half a century later when surfers were body shooting in their hundreds of thousands and incorporating all new kinds of tricks into their repertoire. Williams was able to teach other boys and soon there was a score and more lads at Manly, charging in headlong on the face of the wave, shouting and yelling with the absolute pleasure of it all. Six years after surf shooting began for the first time outside of the small islands of the Pacific, the

The British board riders were not far behind their American counterparts in developing trick riding techniques.

The start of a mass board race paddling for half a dozen miles in the choppy waters of Sydney Harbour. This race in 1965 was won by 17-year-old Nat Young, later to become World Surfboard Champion.

Popularity of the boards began to draw away from the Australian Surf Life Saving movement young athletes such as these.

Australian surf bather who could not shoot a breaker was regarded as only half a surfer 'despised by his fellows; the girls beside him disdain his assistance'.

That 'assistance' sought by the girls in, perhaps, difficulties in the surf, was the prerogative of the 'lifesavers', the Samurais of the surf. Their history is all but the history of the Surf Life Saving Association of Australia, a unique organization which has spread its message of safety on the beaches and its volunteer methods to achieve this safety, to almost every beach area in the world.

Sir Adrian Curlewis, President of the New South Wales Surf Life Saving Association, headed the appeals from the Life Saving movement for the young board riders to amalgamate into the clubs—many of which had trouble at one time finding enough members to keep up patrols.

To be a lifesaver was to be dedicated. A lifesaver's hand showing a rope burn after a day on the lifeline, making rescues in heavy seas.

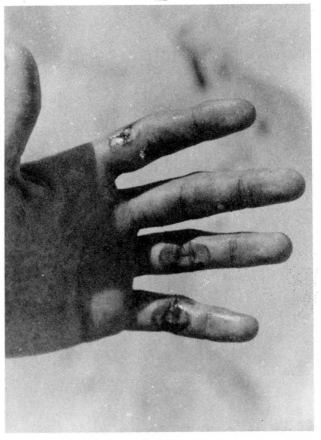

Talented Bobby Brown crouches to protect himself from hitting the board in front—scene, 1961.

The Plastic Machine

Scott Dillon with his huge 'elephant gun' 1962-1963. Note the elaborate fins.

Surf bathing was not all fun. It was a sport that was made for tragedy in those early days, and tragedies there were. The seas off the eastern and western coasts of Australia provide constant waves, rolling in as they do from half way across the world, in the Pacific Ocean on Australia's east coast, and nearly as far in the

Indian Ocean that washes Western Australia's shores. A storm almost anywhere across two thirds of the world builds the waves that eventually crash onto Australia's two main coastlines. So there are occasionally wild surfs springing up in a matter of minutes, and constant rips as the waves that crash onto the Australian shores rush their water back out to sea again. To this situation add the heavy costumes the Australian surfbather was required to wear, and the practice in the early days of the women surfing in one part of the beach and the men in another. That factor was not all puritanism. Clad as they were, the women had no desire to mix with the men, nor were the men in the days before the council regulations on dress, in the best gear for going calling, being like the gentleman in Kipling's verse: 'The raiment that he wore was nothing much before, and rather less than 'alf of that be'ind.' Yet it was ironic that the women, seeking some quiet and unattended corner of the beach in which to dunk themselves

A Sydney female contestant, Sylvia Hoogeveen, appears determined as she turns hard to make points in a local contest in 1965.

About to 'flick off' to end a very good ride.

165

Holding his board hard in trim, Terry Tumeth makes a very frothy wave at South Cronulla Beach, 1961.

Victorian Greg Hill shows his fin as he turns very hard into the water.

in their unlovely clothes, often finished up in difficulties and next awoke to find themselves pulled ashore by some rescuer, lying on the sand having air pumped back into them by some burly stranger, while a few score of the curious stood around and gaped at milady's predicament.

More often than not, these occurrences were not funny at all. Swimming had certainly not developed anywhere near to the point that it

Wayne Lynch—radical re-entry.

Ted Harvey of Sydney showing the unusual fin on his board as he walks up the rocks after a good surf at Angourie, North Coast, New South Wales.

is today and in fact the vast majority of the population of the world were non-swimmers. There were seventeen deaths from drowning on Manly Ocean Beach alone up until 1902 when surfing was only just beginning in the country. With bathers quadrupling, increasing tenfold and more, every month, how many more lives might be lost? Manly again had a first, in deciding to set up several of the installations of the Life Saving Society. This consisted of a pole set dead centre in the middle of the beach from which was hung a coil of rope and a circular lifebuoy. The trouble was that the hemp rope needed little exposure to the salt air and sun to become rotten, while the lifebuoy was of such a size and weight that only the very strongest of swimmers would have any hope of taking it through the breakers to save a life. Indeed, the equipment was worthless, a fact which was demonstrated early

Phil Parkinson at Bellambi Reef, South Coast, N.S.W., trims along a dark wall.

in 1902 at Manly when a young girl, bathing modestly alone, was taken out in a runout. There were good swimmers a hundred yards or more away, but near the girl was only a young man paddling with his family. He went in clothed after her and was also caught in the run-out. His wife's cries for help brought Freddie Williams the surf shooter along, and as much a champion in the surf as he was, he found the weight of the Life Saving Society's buoy far too much for him.

The buoy was taken from him by a local blacksmith, a black-haired young giant named Philip Laurence Daley, who had been taught to surfshoot by Williams. Diving into the run-out he towed the buoy behind him through the breakers, too intent on his task of reaching the struggling pair ahead of him to know that the line on the buoy kept breaking and was being hastily tied together again by helpers on the beach. By the time Daley got out beyond the breaking waves the rope on the buoy was so shortened he could take it no further. He had to return to the beach and both the young girl and the young man who tried to rescue her, were drowned.

Everyone believed that something should be done to see to the safety of those in the surf, but nobody had any answers and the task of saving the lives of those caught in trouble in

South Coast Championship trophies.

With Duke's board behind them at the 1966 Australian Championships—a very young group of well-known surfers. Peter Druyen—Ted Spencer—Kavy—Russell Hughes.

Kevin Platt inside a very fast shorebreak at Collaroy, N.S.W., 1966.

Frank Latta head dips on the Cronulla
shorebreak, N.S.W.

Behind the baths at Collaroy, N.S.W.,
Bob McTavish coaxing his board for
maximum speed to make the wave.

the surf continued to be anybody's job for
many years until Manly appointed the first
official lifesaver in Australia, Edward 'Happy'
Eyre, a genial New Zealander who had carried
out many rescues in the Manly surf as a
volunteer since the 1890s. On 15 October,
1907, the Manly Council made his job an
official one on salary, but the days of Manly as
a trendsetter were about over. Eyre was not
the forerunner of a huge system of paid
official lifesavers on Australian beaches. In the
very same year events were moving that would
set up the most unusual organization perhaps
the world has seen, a completely voluntary
organization which, from its inception in 1908

up until the present day has saved the staggering
total of nearly a quarter million lives on
beaches all around Australia—The Surf Life
Saving Association of Australia.
The haphazard attempts at life saving that
had gone on at Manly had been duplicated at
every other beach in the Sydney area. No one
had proper equipment, no one knew anything
of the methods required to save life in the surf.
The Life Saving Society had its branches at
several beach centres, but its methods were
worked out overseas and were designed for
saving life in still water conditions. Something
had to be done, and done quickly as more and
more budding surfers drowned in the rips and

John Coleman powers in a turn at Bellambi, South Coast, N.S.W., 1963.

Bobby Brown tears into a spectacular backhand turn on the shore break at Apollo Bay, Victoria, 1964.

Phil Parkinson arches into a stylish turn
at Bellambi, South Coast, N.S.W.

Early morning cutback from Wayne
Williams as he silhouettes against his
foam at Angourie, N.S.W.

Fantastic turn of speed from Terry Fitzgerald as he tears his way along a Kirra wave in Queensland.

crashing waves of the beaches. It was at this time that Lyster Ormsby emerged as the father of the methods to save the drowning at sea which are still in general use today. Ormsby, with Percy Flynn and Sid Fullwood, had been amongst the leaders in a group of Bondi surfers who had got together to fight the prosecution of the Rector of St. Mary's, Waverley, when he was charged with bathing in prohibited hours. That same group of dissidents were all regular bathers at Bondi and had been trained in the Life Saving Society's methods of rescue and treatment of the drowning. They formed themselves in 1906, into the Bondi Surf Bathers' Life Saving Club and almost immediately began working on the special problems facing the swimmer in difficulties in the ocean surf, and how best to rescue him. The club's first premises was a tent given them

on loan but within a year they had a room on the beachfront, lent to the group by the Waverley Council. The club members patrolled their beach every weekend on a volunteer basis and were able to report after their first season that things had gone satisfactorily and no lives had been lost while the patrols were on duty. The extraordinary

The Surfing Set.

Bob McTavish forces his way through a very tight section at Angourie, N.S.W.

Cutting back into the wave to gain more power—Bob McTavish tears in on an 8 foot wave at Angourie, North Coast, N.S.W.

fact is that until the present day, after the formation of hundreds of other surf life saving clubs and the setting up of the parent body, the Surf Life Saving Association of Australia, that same proud boast can be made—'no lives lost while patrols were on duty'—and that after a quarter million rescues!

The biggest problem facing Ormsby and his colleagues was proper lifesaving gear. To get someone in difficulties from the surf had first been a matter of a bunch of spectators holding

hands in a human chain, which had obvious and severe limitations. Then there came the hemp ropes and lifebuoys which had proven so useless, followed by a rope attached to a ship's lifejacket, which also proved unsatisfactory in that the rescuer taking the jacket out in heavy seas was unable to dive under the incoming waves because of the jacket's bulk and buoyancy. The fact that the lifesaving gear was fixed in one position on the beach was another major drawback, for the individualist Australian was inclined to swim just where he pleased, which as often as not was as far away as could be from the lifesaving gear. So Ormsby and his colleagues dreamed up the plan of having a rescue line on a portable reel which could be moved quickly to any part of the beach. Together with Flynn and Warrant Officer John Bond of the Royal Australian Medical Corps, Ormsby worked out his ideas with a cotton reel and a couple of hairpins, drew up a rough

On an 18 foot Bells Beach wave (Victoria) Bob McTavish powers his way through . . .

. . . crouches low to gain more momentum, but ended up 'eating' water for a very bad wipe-out.

175

plan on a Vanity Fair cigarette packet and then turned the whole thing over to Oldings, the local coachbuilders and the result was the first surf reel, the first of thousands of such reels now in service all over the world, saving life from Palestine to Peru, wherever men and women go down to the sea to surf.

Ormsby also worked out a method and style of rescue using the reel to which military man Bond added the drill and polish and thus set up the fundamental system of Rescue and Resuscitation that is the keystone of all rescue work in the Australian surf today. The first public demonstration of the new reel was given on Bondi Beach on 23 December 1906 and only eleven days later it was used in a rescue of some significance. Two small boys were washed out in a rip and the lifesavers went out after them, attached to the reel by rope and cork belt. The first lad brought in was in a serious condition and couldn't speak for some time. When he had recovered sufficiently he gave his name as Charlie Smith, of Yates Street, North Sydney. Charlie Smith

had beaten the sea on that occasion, but it was to get him in the end. For that same Charlie Smith grew up to be Sir Charles Kingsford Smith, who thirty years later, after proving himself as one of the world's greatest pioneer airmen and making of himself an Australian national hero, came down in the sea on an England-Australia flight, and was never seen again.

Very quickly after the lead set by Bondi, and an earlier group of lifesaving enthusiasts at nearby Bronte, surf clubs were set up by swimmers at all the main beaches and on 18 October 1907 surfers from all the clubs

Danny Bond head dips under a curl for a spectacular ride.

176

Colin Smith does a complete change of direction (start of the 360° turn) to finish with a re-entry, 1969.

Wayne Williams tears into a forehand turn at Noosa Heads, Queensland.

Ted Spencer, with perfect control, re-enters in the Bobby Brown Championships, at Cronulla, N.S.W.

Port Kembla, N.S.W., surfer pushes hard inside the tube in an effort to make the wave.

Peter Druyen locked in a Coolangatta wave in the 1966 Australian Championships. He won the Junior Title.

gathered at the Sydney Sports Club to form the Surf Bathers' Association of New South Wales. It was a most successful and happy meeting, and one of the main items on the agenda was a matter that was doing much to foster consolidation and concerted action on the part of the otherwise individualistic surfers. It was at this time that the Mayors of Waverley, Randwick and Manly were demanding that surfers, men and women alike, wear skirts on their neck-to-knee costumes for the sake of propriety. The brawny surfers were aghast at the prospect of being made to dress like their womenfolk, condemned the idea at that first meeting of the Surf Bathers' Association and soon afterwards took part in a protest march from Bondi Beach into the city—and an hilarious protest march it must have been, for the brawny surfers were dressed in their sisters' petticoats, in skirts made of old chaff bags, in the weirdest assortment of clothing that fulfilled the council demands for 'a skirt' and

Perfectly positioned, 'Butch' Cooney trims along the shorebreak at Newcastle Beach, N.S.W., in the Newcastle Championships, 1967.

A very young 'Butch' Cooney rips into a backhand turn at Collaroy, N.S.W., 1965.

In 1964 some of the younger surfers at Maroubra, N.S.W.

Three finalists in the 1963 Australian titles at Bondi Beach—Bob Kenneson, Mick Dooley, John 'Wheels' Williams.

Goofy foot rider Gary Birdsall trimming beautifully inside a wall at Cronulla Point, N.S.W., 1963.

everyone else's need for a good laugh, to the full. In the face of such ridicule, no more was heard of the 'skirts for all bathers' issue. These groups of young men who formed the first volunteer surf lifesaving clubs soon threw up their own heroes, their 'chief Samurais'. One of the first was Harald Baker who excelled at all sports and who was the most powerful of all the swimmers on the Australian beaches. He was one of the founders of the Maroubra Surf Lifesaving Club and it was his name that was invariably shouted out whenever a surfer got into trouble on that beach. He scorned the use of the lifebelt and reel and went out on his rescues singlehanded, yet he had totted up 100 rescues from the booming and treacherous Maroubra surf before 1910, when he moved further up the coast to Coogee Beach. There, during January 1911, he and international footballer and surfer, Jimmy Clarken figured in the first mass rescue ever made in the surf.

Coogee Beach featured a stormwater drain running into the beach, gouging out a great hole in the sea. After a week of heavy rain this hole was twenty feet wide and the same depth and so created a tremendous backwash.

Jeff O'Lachlan grabs the 'rail' for tighter trim, to make a critical wave at Voodoo, Kurnell, N.S.W.

181

Ray Cook surfing in the 1961 Australian Championships at Bondi Beach, N.S.W.

Jack Eden on the nose at Port Kembla, N.S.W., 1960.

Baker put a red flag in the sand opposite the hole, but this was ignored by a bunch of young factory hands who had been let off work early and who had come down to the beach to enjoy themselves. They went into the water well to the north of the danger area and enjoyed themselves so much they failed to notice they were being steadily washed towards that danger hole. The great majority of the Coogee Surf Club members on this day were off at a surf carnival at North Steyne and only Baker and his mate Clarken were about, fully dressed, yarning in front of the small refreshment kiosk Baker ran on the beach. Then, in a matter of moments, thirteen of the happy party of surfers had been sucked into that deep hole and were struggling for their lives. Baker didn't wait to pull off his clothes but ran to the danger area, grabbed a belt while Clarken worked the reel and went into the surf. The struggling young men and women grabbed for him when he reached them, and with waves pounding on top of them, Baker could only knock out one girl and fight off three others before heading back to the beach dragging three sodden girls with him. Before going back in after more struggling girls and young men, Baker stripped to the buff, then swam out again to bring in the thirteen, most of them unconscious. Then he and Clarken worked to resuscitate the limp bodies lying a

182

Looking up, watching the wave about to collapse, a young surfer speeds to avoid a wipeout.

One of Australia's leading surfers, Frank Latta, shows the way in 1970, with a very fast backhand turn.

The small boards of 1970 are used to the maximum. This surfer shows how as he takes off.

over the sand. Four men failed to revive; the job had been too big for just two men. But good was to come of this, for the tragedy led to a revision of beach patrol arrangements and the Surf Bathers' Association drafted new rules insisting that regular Saturday afternoon patrols of at least seven men should be in attendance on all beaches wherever a surf club functioned, and the same rules apply today. Baker was regarded as even more of a hero than he had been before the tragedy, but that was small consolation for the fact that one irate bystander at the rescue wrote to a newspaper declaring his disgust that Baker had performed his rescue and his resuscitation efforts completely naked. And if that wasn't enough,

Going for top trim to make the wave a young surfer speeds out of the white water.

Frank Latta rips through the white water, 1970.

while Baker was in the sea, some thief rifled the till in his kiosk! However, a public subscription raised more than one thousand pounds as a testimonial to Baker's bravery, and he was also awarded the Albert Medal, the highest civilian award made for acts of outstanding heroism.

The publicity associated with exploits such as Baker's attracted more and more young men to the young surfing movement. The idea was quickly brought about that it was an honour to be accepted as a lifesaver and there was never any question of the young men being paid for the work that they did in saving lives, often at great risk to their own. But the tradition having been set, it has never been

Bells Beach, Victoria, 1964. Sitting on the surfboard are Nat Young, Mick Dooley and Nipper Williams. Midget on the right.

broken and ever since the lifesaving movement has been a purely voluntary affair, with aspiring lifesavers being required to pay a subscription to the club they wish to join, then undergoing a severe swimming test, being placed on probation to train and study for the Bronze Medallion of efficiency in surf rescue work. Only then can he call himself a lifesaver and give up his weekends to patrolling the beaches, or helping with functions to raise the $6,000 or more to outfit his club with the most basic equipment for carrying out rescue and patrol work. It is a labour of love, it has been said, but certainly it is the most unusual

organization the world can show, and it all began out of the hearts, minds and muscle of those handful of Australian beach pioneers at the start of the century. Within two or three years those first lifesavers had made feats of heroism on Australian beaches as commonplace as the sun that came up every day.

The biggest and strongest of the generally big and strong Australian young men were attracted to the lifesaving clubs, and the lifesaver fast got the reputation of being something of a superman. So Australians were pleased rather than surprised at the athletic feats of men such as Harold Hardwick, a

With a watery roof above him, a surfer slides along a long wall.

A surfer paddles out in the silver water to commence his 'thing' for the day.

Balsa boards from the 1959-60 era—note the large fins and turn-up at the back.

Australian Championships at Bondi, 1961.
John O'Donovan up front.

Speed! Terry Fitzgerald.

Local Cronulla, N.S.W., bellyboard rider
screams into the turn of a point wave.

lifesaver with the Manly Club who, in 1909 equalled the Australian 100 yards swim time of 57 seconds, and so won selection in the Australian team for the first Empire Games, held in London in 1911. Hardwick, who was also a boxer, won the 100 yards freestyle title at that meet and the next night knocked out two opponents—with only an hour's rest between fights—to win the heavyweight boxing title of the British Empire.

Hardwick stood a half inch over six feet and weighed only 11 stone 11 lbs. Yet he disposed of his first opponent, a 13 stone 7 lb. policeman, William Hazell, heavyweight champion of Scotland and England, in only 2 minutes 33 seconds, the referee having to stop the fight. After an hour's rest, Hardwick was back in the ring again against another policeman, Thompson, the Canadian champion. Thompson lasted exactly two seconds longer

John 'Nipper' Williams.

Amazing control through a fast head dip.

than Hazell before the referee stopped the fight because Hardwick wouldn't hit his helpless opponent further.

Before he came back to Australia from that trip, Hardwick won the 110, 220 and 440 yards freestyle championships of England and the 100 metres championship of Germany. The next year he went to the 1912 Olympics in Stockholm in the Australasian swimming team which won the 800 metres relay in world

189

Balanced expertly on his surfboard, a
North Bondi lifesaver coasts shoreward
on the crest of a Pacific roller.

record time. Hardwick swam to bronze medals for third place in the 400 metres and the 1500 metres. When war broke out in 1914 Hardwick joined up and rose from the ranks to become a Colonel, was the British Forces heavyweight boxing champion and in 1919 won the British-awarded trophy as Ideal Sportsman of the Empire. Hardwick also played first grade Rugby Union in Sydney from 1908 to 1913, representing the state of New South Wales against a visiting American side in 1910.

That was the kind of man that attracted Australians in their tens of thousands down to the beaches to watch these magnificent athletes just walk around, or carry out their surf drills. The best looking girls were always to be found where the lifesavers' enclosure was. So it followed that to win a young girl's heart, it was a great idea to be a lifesaver, and the volunteer movement prospered further. Not that the young surfing movement was a bunch of film stars posturing and posing. The authority was strong, the discipline strict, the whole movement aimed at one thing and one thing only—saving lives in the surf.

While the pioneers were discarding the old fashioned equipment and substituting their

L. to r.: Nat Young (Australia), Mike Doyle (U.S.A.), Midget Farrelly (Australia), Joey Cabell (U.S.A.), and Linda Bensen (U.S.A.). 1964 World Title winners.

World Titles 1964

Framed by a local surf boat, Joey Cabell walks along his board for maximum speed—World Titles 1964.

Australian Titles, 1964: Midget Farrelly 1st, Nat Young 2nd, Bob McTavish 3rd. This was run in conjunction with world titles.

Mike Doyle drives on the nose to show the style which placed him second in the World Titles, 1964.

Fantastic hard backhand turn by Mike Doyle (U.S.A.).

own inventions such as the reel, to enable the lifesavers to get out into the surf and haul their patients back to shore, there was still the problem of reviving the unconscious and the apparently drowned. At the turn of the century the resuscitation methods of a certain Dr. Hall were in vogue, taken from a pamphlet he wrote entitled 'How to promote breathing by exciting the nostrils with snuff, hartshorn or volatile salts or by tickling the throat with a feather.'

Better practices were taught by the naval surgeons of the time but their experiences and teachings were confined within the service and did not get into public use. The naval surgeons should have known quite a lot about resuscitation from drowning, since most British sailors in those days were non-swimmers for one thing, but particularly because one of the favourite disciplinary methods in use in the British Navy was the practice of keelhauling, where a sailor to be punished was tied to a rope and passed down one side of his ship, under the bottom and up the other side. One Naval surgeon, James Lind, in 1757, advised that the apparently drowned should not be hung up by the heels to drain, but should be laid down and wrapped in blankets, 'the limbs should be chafed while an assistant—preferably one who chewed garlic—blows into the mouth. At the same time another person, by alternate gentle pressure and dilation of the ribs, with a corresponding alternate compression of the contents of the

Young junior surfer blows out as he turns into his cutback—at the World Titles, 1964.

193

Layout of the heats, first day—
Manly, N.S.W.

Beautiful trimming by Wayne Burton in the
finals of the World Titles, 1964.

belly upwards, is to be directed to imitate, as nearly as possible the act of respiration in the human body'.

Lind was certainly on the right track, though the garlic is not considered these days to be altogether necessary. Yet it was not until 1908 that Professor Schafer, of Edinburgh University, sent his methods of resuscitation to the Coogee Surf Club in Australia, on request. In the Schafer method the patient is placed face downwards in a prone position, the head being lower than the body, in which position the tongue falls naturally forward clear of the windpipe. The resuscitator then takes up a position with his right leg between the legs of the prone patient and, with his hands placed slightly above the small of the back, the heels of his hands resting on the lowest ribs, alternately exerts and releases a careful pressure at a uniform rate of twelve

complete movements or pumps, to the minute. Resuscitators were advised to persevere with this movement for at least three hours, in relays if necessary, and there is the famous reply of a budding lifesaver asked during his Bronze Medallion examination how long he should continue to pump at a patient: 'Until life is pronounced extinct by a doctor, and then for half an hour afterwards.'

That method of resuscitation was the basis of

A most unusual angle shows three waves coming in—while being watched by a surfer paddling out—another surfer drops inside the second wave and crosses the trail of another surfer hidden from view. Note the trails of the two riders on the wave. World Titles, 1964.

Joey Cabell, one of the best board riders in the world, hangs ten in the 1964 finals.

the Australian lifesaver's work for forty years until the 'breath of life' system was introduced as an improvement. But for all the years between the Australian lifesaver drilled with his team of linemen, belt swimmer, reel men and 'patient', carrying out practice rescues where the 'patient' swam out more than 100 yards from shore, raised his arm in the traditional signal for help. The scamper of beltman to belt and into the surf, the linemen paying out the line, the patient reached, the arm raised again for the haul in, the dash into the shore break by the linemen when the beltman was able to stand in the shallows, the hoisting of the patient face downwards, legs raised, on the shoulders of the strapping linemen, the resuscitation on the beach; this became as common a sight to the Australian surfer as the policeman on point duty, directing traffic.

Improvements were made in equipment as the lifesavers hardened their experience. The ship's lifejacket instead of the cumbersome lifebuoy was itself replaced by a cork-filled belt which most lifesavers didn't like because of its buoyancy, then years later came the thin canvas belt which is still in use today, modified by tragic experience to include a safety unlocking device developed in New Zealand. Prior to the safety pin release,

Left.
Part of the 30,000 people who watched
the 1964 World Titles at Manly Beach.

Below left.
Layout of Championships, Manly, N.S.W.

Kimo Hollinger emerges from a hairy ride
at the inside break at Sunset Beach,
Hawaii. Three surfers are almost obscured
by the white water behind him.
See page 200 for the scene a few seconds
before.

Making a Board

One of Sydney's top shapers, Laurie Burns, starts to plane the blank after roughing it out with a hand-saw—the blank is made of poly-urethane foam poured into a pressure mould.

After shaping and fine sand-papering, surfer Brian Jackson checks the various custom-made shapes against his order form.

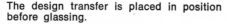

The design transfer is placed in position before glassing.

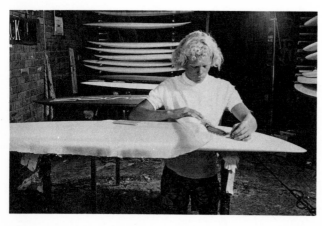

lifesavers had drowned when huge patches of seaweed washed over their line, dragging them under the water, and one man had been held helpless in his belt while a shark tore him to pieces.

All this practice and improvement, research and testing was carried out by the volunteers themselves. For more than thirty years, their work was simply accepted by all and sundry. The local councils offered no help in accommodation and chicken coops and huts went up as clubhouses until reluctant councils after years of prodding agreed to provide dressing shed accommodation for the public, and squeeze in some rooms on the plans for the lifesavers' clubhouse as well. The public equally took the lifesavers for granted, for instance during 1937 approximately 500 major rescues were carried out by lifesavers on Bondi, North Bondi and Manly beaches alone, from which about a dozen letters of thanks were received and one or two donations—and this to clubs which each had to find the money to buy their own equipment, right down to the first aid man who had to supply more bandages and sticking plaster to surfers in a day than a doctor in a thriving practice would use in a week.

Such gods, the public seemed to reason, needed no help from the public. But the public certainly needed the help of the lifesavers. And no more so than on the afternoon of 6 February 1938, at Bondi Beach, a day which has gone down in Australian surfing history as Black Sunday. Carl Jeppeson was captain of the

The actual fibreglassing, done with special laminating resin.

After the build-up coat of resin is applied the 'grinder' works off all the excess resin to a smooth finish—it is sandpapered and then given a final coat of resin.

The board is buffed to a high gloss.

Kimo Hollinger locked in the inside break at Sunset Beach, Hawaii, while Paul Gaebuer, Kit Horn and Rusty Miller drop down the face of a big one outside. See what happened on Page 197.

Dewey Weber on the nose at Sunset Beach, Hawaii.

Bondi Club at that time, and he remembers Black Sunday in these words:

'It looked like being a typical Sydney summer Sunday at Bondi. Already, at 8 a.m. as I made my way to the surf club house, men, women and children were arriving, singly and in groups. The sun had an early sting to it and a good surf was running, with waves breaking evenly about 100 yards off shore. On the beach, the early morning patrol was on guard.

'For the next couple of hours, club members drifted in, but there was more to do than just talk—teams to be drilled, test times to be taken, new members to be interviewed, visitors to be welcomed. And we had a problem in that we had to go through the difficulties of clearing part of the thickly crowded beach for the start and finish of our regular surf race. The race being on, it meant we had to use the club's one available surf boat to moor the buoys off shore and to stand by them, when the boat might be urgently required elsewhere.

'That race was never held that day. As the day passed the waves grew bigger and developed a lot more kick in them until now and then an unwary surfer would stick up his or her arm and a rescue team would go in and pull them out. By then, the number of people on the beach and in the water had grown to about

35,000. We had one bit of luck, though. Just after 3 p.m. the fellows from the new patrol had come in to the club to relieve those who had been on duty earlier in the day and some sixty more lifesavers were heading down to the beach for the start of the surf race.

'Then it happened. Several large, broken waves rolled to the shore. They were probably no bigger than those which had gone before but they followed in quick succession and a number of bathers, standing on a sandbank about sixty yards out, found themselves out of their depth. Hands shot up for help. We weren't alarmed, for it was a normal type of thing, a rescue our patrol could safely handle and its members were already on their way out to the swimmers.

'But worse was to follow. Previously that day, the waves had reached the shore and receded separately. But the quick waves in succession had combined to form one huge mass of water, which, as it receded seawards, swept

Midget Farrelly

Midget Farrelly backhand turns and . . .

Taken from the water at Angourie, N.S.W.
Midget's turn is watched by John
O'Donovan as he paddles out.

hundreds of surfers from the sandbank into a deep, adjacent channel, and those already in trouble further out to sea.

'From then on, it was just hell, men, women and children fighting for their lives. It was mass hysteria at its worst. In frenzy they shouted, screamed, cried, begged and prayed. They grabbed, clawed and fought while some calmer surfers tried to reassure and help them. On the beach there was a stunned, but shortlived silence. This just couldn't be true.

'But it was. And, in another instant, those lifesavers ready for competition against each other were on their way in a greater race— against time and death. They manned the available surf reels, seven in all, grabbed up any rubber surf float, surf board or ski in sight or swam strongly towards the turmoil with only their surfing skill to help them.

'While there was incredible hysteria in the surf there was also mass panic on the beach as people frantically sought relatives and friends

. . . water flies as he drives his board
at maximum speed.

In the State titles in 1965 Midget's control
is demonstrated here as he goes hard left.

Midget started a trend in the 1964 world
titles (which he won) when he rode the
first stringerless board—here he rips into
the shorebreak on this new type of
board.

Midget Farrelly hanging ten at Angourie—
a hot spot in Northern N.S.W.

Page 204
Makaha Championships, Hawaii. Midget
Farrelly, representing Australia, races to
beat the curl off Makaha Point closely
followed by Conrad Cunha of Hawaii.

A very fast cutback at Kirra, Queensland—1970 style—Midget.

Arriving home fresh from winning 1963 Makaha Championships, Midget bottom turns at Narrabeen, N.S.W.

'Rail' turn at Dee Why, N.S.W., above, and then driving through, below.

and rushed the surf lines, breaking one, and inexpertly hauling the beltmen under water or before patients were properly secured. The police had been quickly called but neither they nor the calmer members of the public could cope with the situation and we had to send out radio appeals for more police, doctors and ambulances.

'In the surf the melee grew worse as more heavy, broken waves broke over the gasping victims and their intending rescuers. The lifesavers had to make quick decisions as to who most needed help and then fight off the others who also wanted saving. People were sinking all around us as we tried to get them to surf floats, to hold them up, to calm them.

'Never will I forget the appealing blue eyes of a curly, blond youngster of about eight years or so, or his cry of 'Save me, mister' when he swept past me as I struggled towards the beach with two elderly women. That feeling of complete helplessness I shall never forget, and it was relieved only when I later found that boy was not among those lost.

'Naturally, it had been women and children first and all these were saved. Rescue operations continued as lifesavers brought ashore patients in varying stages of unconsciousness and returned to the surf again, for more and more. Outside the break of the waves, our surfboat

Nat Young 'on edges' a very tight turn at Long Reef, N.S.W.

was standing helpless. It would have been disastrous for it to have come in any closer to try and assist.

'After about thirty minutes the water seemed to have been cleared. There was no one in sight in the turmoil of foam but we were frightened at just how many victims there might be dead on the bottom. Amazingly—as we found out later—there was only one.

'Of the estimated 250 surfers in difficulties, only a handful had got back to the beach by themselves. The rest we had dragged in. But the job was far from over. On the sand were lying about seventy victims, at least thirty of them unconscious and near to death. Some order had been restored, but there were still many frantic people trying to find children, mothers, fathers and friends as doctors, ambulancemen and surfers worked to resuscitate the victims.

'For two hours we worked on them seeing miracles, as apparently hopeless, blackfaced patients were restored to life. But four of the men we brought ashore could not be revived and a fifth victim was recovered from the water's edge five days later.'

It was dark when Jeppeson and his colleagues left Bondi Beach on that day after sorting out unclaimed clothing in case they belonged to other victims still beneath the waves, after making their reports and answering hundreds of telephone calls from worried relatives and friends who had heard of the tragedy on the radio. On that day Bondi lost its proud record of thirty-two years standing, of no lives lost while patrols were on duty, but in the records of the lifesaving movement that spread around the world in later years, Bondi's 'Black Sunday' rescue is still regarded as its greatest mass achievement.

The vigorous surf of the Australian beaches, the sudden flare-ups of rips and undertows and giant, dumping waves, was not the only worry for the volunteer lifesavers, however. The surf they knew. Today on Sydney beaches there is an average of fifty rescues of surfers in trouble every weekend. That is the lifesaver's job. He knows it and is used to it. But he doesn't know and certainly will never get used to the great unknown danger that threatens surfers all over the world—the shark.

On all evidence collected of shark attacks around the world since 1920 it appears that at any given time of the year the shark attack

George Downing's surf shop on the beach at Waikiki, Hawaii.

Butch Van Artsdalen sliding along the face of a beautiful transparent wave at Nanikai, Hawaii.

Running along the top at tremendous speed. Nat prepares to bottom turn at Long Reef.

The 'animal' literally ripping the waves apart in the 1968 Australian Championship.

belt around the world is approximately 4,000 miles wide, which accounts for a lot of popular surfing beaches. But by far the worst area in the world for shark attacks on surfers is in Australia, on the eastern coast, where the sharks are considered to be the most vicious in the world. South African surfers have also had to live and die with sharks, which also swarm off that country's eastern coast. In both countries attacks occur between similar latitudes. In both countries a warm current sweeps down the eastern coast in a southerly curve. In both countries the east coast has similar

drainage and sewage outfalls in the attack areas. Paradoxically Australia's neighbor, New Zealand, has a seasonal zone record of shark attacks almost as good as Australia's is bad. All of New Zealand's North Island and about one third of the South Island lie within the southern seasonal zone. The western coast of the United States has had less than one third as many attacks as has the eastern coast and all of these have occurred off one state, California. In all these attacks the estimation of how dangerous lifesaving operations on shark victims were, was assessed and in a list of cases where

Nat Young's beautiful control is shown here in Australian Titles, 1968.

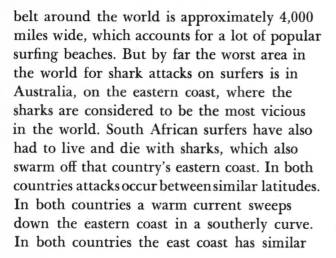

The 'animal', Nat Young, tears into a turn.

Surfing very tightly at Collaroy, N.S.W. Nat Young.

Nat Young drives deep into a backhand turn at the World Titles, 1964.

Former American world champion surfboard rider, Joyce Hoffman, riding high on the curl at Pupakea, Hawaii.

The shape and the style in Tahiti.

Mark Martinson from California runs along the top of a beautiful wall at Haleiwa, Hawaii.

only one person was available to help the victim, eleven rescuers were attacked and thirty-nine were not. Where two persons were available to help, not one of eighteen rescuers was attacked. Where more than two persons helped at once not one of seven rescuers was attacked.

But these slightly comforting statistics were not in the hands of the Australian lifesavers who swam out unarmed and unprotected in blood soaked seas to pull victims from the jaws

of shark after shark in the early days of Australian surfing. These lifesaver heroes were not to know in those days, either, that the eastern seaboard of Australia has experienced more shark attacks than any other region of comparable size in the world.

A wave of shark attack hysteria swept Sydney when two surfers were fatally mauled within a month of each other at Coogee Beach in 1922. The victims were Milton Singleton Coughlan, eighteen years of age, a member of the Coogee

Lifesaving Club, and twenty-one-year-old Mervyn Gannon. Coughlan, the son of the Randwick postmaster was a top athlete. He had figured in the rescue of a surfer at nearby Maroubra Beach only the week before he was attacked by one of three sharks that were seen from the beach.

Coughlan was farthest out of a group of surfers when he suddenly screamed 'shark, shark' and began flailing the water. The shark, described as being comparatively small, attacked again and again, snapping away the young man's fists as he fought it, stripping his arms of flesh from shoulders to spouting wrists. Surfers on the clubhouse verandah were dumbfounded with horror for a moment, then lifesaver Jack Chalmers charged into the surf and swam out to Coughlan.

Chalmers described the rescue later: 'When I

Even at this early age Nat Young shows the aggressiveness which was to characterize his style years later.

A very young Nat Young driving from a radical turn at Dee Why Point, N.S.W.

Nat Young about to enter the water at Collaroy, 1962.

Surfing from the 'chair' at Dee Why Point, N.S.W., Nat Young.

Nat Young, Bells Beach, Victoria.

Local Wollongong girl, Lyn Stubbins, executes a classy backhand turn at Bellambi Reef, New South Wales.

reached him the shark was still tugging at one of his arms and the water was stained with blood. Yet he managed to turn his back toward me in the position as practised in our life saving drill. He said to me "hang on to me tightly".

'Then he collapsed and the shark let him go.' Frank Beaurepaire, later to represent Australia in Olympic Games swimming, also swam out to help and he and Chalmers brought Coughlan to shore, where he died. Chalmers became a national hero overnight. Married, with three children and not in regular employment, many thousands of pounds were raised for him in tribute to his bravery. As well, he was awarded the Albert Medal, the highest civilian award for bravery, and the Surfer's V.C.—the Meritorious Award in Silver—awarded only in cases deemed to be characterized by bravery far beyond what is considered the ordinary duty of a lifesaver.

While the public was still trembling with the shock of the attack on Coughlan, less than a month later Mervyn Gannon was attacked at

Victorian Wayne Lynch has left his mark on the surfing scene, with his 360° turn and radical re-entries.

Judy Trim. Won Australian Titles, 1968, and State Titles, 1968 and 1969.

The Innovators

Coogee while swimming only twenty-five yards from the shore in shallow water. Horrified onlookers saw Gannon hit at the shark with his right arm and when it came out of the water, there was only a bleeding stump of it left.

Beach inspector John Brown and a bystander Ernest Carter rushed into the water and pulled Gannon towards the shore, with the shark still attacking. The horribly mauled man told Brown: 'I'm dead stiff, Brownie. If there had been fourteen sharks out there they would

Midget Farrelly, first surfboard riding champion of the world in 1964. One time title holder of Australian National Surfboard Riding Championship, Makaha Championship, South African Professional Invitation Surfboard Riding Championship and the small wave section of the world titles in Peru.

One of the best surfing photographers in the world. Dr Don James, an American dentist, coming in from Sunset after a day's 'shooting'.

Dr Don James on a Sunset wave.

The incredible Bobby Brown, who was the idol of many surfers, shows the style which won him much acclaim at Sandon Point, N.S.W.

'Snow' McAlister, famous for his board riding headstands, is an active and enthusiastic organizer of surfboard riding events.

Bob Evans, movie-maker, talking to world-renowned surfers Scott Dillon and Bob Pike.

Robert Connelly, one of Australia's best surfers, won the Australian Junior Title and was a finalist in the Australian Titles for many years.

have all had a bite of me.' His right hand had been bitten off, the left hand was so badly mutilated most of it would have had to be amputated, but the main injuries were to the lower part of his back.

In hospital later he told a relative: 'I saw the shark when it was about ten yards away from me. As it came in I managed to jump on it, but like a flash it slithered away from underneath me and as I tried to punch it away it grabbed my right hand. It was an awful feeling, but I managed to get on a little breaking wave that carried me along towards the shore. The shark came at me again. I tried my left on him this time but it was no good, he got me again. Then Brownie and the other chap reached me. We were getting along nicely when the shark tore at my back. I thought my heart would stop beating, but we managed to get in.'

Despite his incredible courage, Gannon died in hospital and a nine foot blue pointer shark was blamed. Rewards were offered for any

219

MIDGET FARRELLY SHOWS HOW

Top row: Midget Farrelly's perfect control is illustrated here as he applies pressure to the back rail before dropping down the front of the wave.

Centre row: Midget rips through white water as he completes a re-entry.

Bottom row: (Right to left) This is the 1967 style of the former world champion as he drops down the face of a wave, stalls, hangs five, trims and completes a well controlled manoeuvre.

shark caught off Coogee, higher rewards being offered for the shark that had killed the two young men. A man had disappeared, presumed taken by a shark at Bilgola, one of Sydney's northern beaches only a few days before Gannon's death, so Sydney was full of shark talk. Many beaches were all but deserted because of the fear of being taken. Idea after idea was put forward on how to end the shark terror.

On 12 March one of the most incredible sights seen off a Sydney beach took place when nine Loyalty Islanders visiting the city, armed themselves with sheath knives and marlin spikes and swam into the Coogee breakers to do battle with the sharks. Eighty thousand spectators jammed the beach and cliffs hoping to see a bloody battle between man and the surf killers, but the Islanders failed to sight one shark, despite that they had hours before suspended shark baits from floats nearly 100 yards from shore.

Shark attacks continued to occur up and down the eastern Australian surfing beaches, gaining for the country a fearsome reputation abroad, and pressure mounted on the authorities to find a way to abate the menace. The public fear reached its greatest heights in October 1937 when a shark killed not one man, but two, off Kirra Beach, at Coolangatta, on the New South Wales-Queensland border.

It was an incredibly savage attack. In a short

John 'Wheels' Williams crouches inside a beautiful curl.

Scott Dillon about to be 'eaten' by a large wave at Fairy Bower, Sydney.

space of time late in the afternoon, Norman Girvan, eighteen years of age, and Jack Brinkley, twenty-five years, were mauled so severely that one died in the water and the other soon after having his arm amputated. At the time of the attack seven swimmers were in a group on a sandbank about 200 yards from the beach at 5.30 p.m. Three of the group—Norman Girvan, Jack Brinkley and Gordon Doniger, began swimming ashore. About 100 yards from the beach, they reached a channel near another sandspit.

Doniger and Girvan, only a few yards apart, were joking about sharks when suddenly Girvan cried out: 'Quick, Don, a shark's got me.' Doniger thought Girvan was still joking

Bob Evans, local movie and magazine producer, surfing at Coolangatta, Queensland.

Brian Jackson, a board builder, trims inside a beautiful wave at Sand Shoes Beach, N.S.W.

223

until the youth put up his arm and Doniger could see that blood was everywhere. Girvan called out: 'It won't let go. It's got my leg.' Doniger said later that when he reached Girvan and held him he felt the youth being violently shaken about until, to his horror, Girvan was pulled from his grip.

The shark surfaced. It was a large one. Girvan said: 'I'm gone. Goodbye.' Almost immediately the shark dragged him under. Doniger said that as he was swimming over to help Girvan he saw Jack Brinkley nearby and called to him for help. But just as Brinkley started to swim towards Doniger he was also attacked. On the beach Joseph Doniger saw the attacks and went into the surf to swim out to his brother and Girvan. As he swam he saw Brinkley

attacked and he went to him and brought him ashore. On the way in, the shark bit Brinkley again, grabbing him by the left arm below the shoulder. Severe lacerations ran up and down Brinkley's side and his left arm was almost torn off. In Coolangatta hospital he was given massive blood transfusions and his arm was amputated, but he died shortly afterwards. Determined efforts were made to catch the shark and on the day after the attack a tiger shark nearly twelve feet long was caught. When the shark's stomach was opened it was found to contain portions of undigested arms and legs. It was possible to identify, by a scar, that a right hand in the stomach was Girvan's. The wound on Brinkley's left arm above the elbow was clean, as though it had been cut with

Girl surfer catapulting through the shorebreak at Makaha Beach, Hawaii.

Buzzy Trent driving from the top of a huge Waimea Bay wall as a rider below heads for the safety of a wipeout.

Two belly board riders having fun as they skip down the face of a wave at Cronulla Point, N.S.W.

Midget Farrelly, Nat Young and Ted Spencer.

a sharp knife while the wound on the forearm was about five inches long, neither clean nor ragged. It was theorized later that there was only one shark involved in the attack and that its target was Girvan. As it sped by its fin and body brushed Brinkley with such tremendous force it inflicted the terrible wounds upon him. There were many such attacks, all of them fully reported in the Press and the authorities obviously had to do something about sharks. But what? Crackpots had a field day and some of the suggestions put to the Government included clothing all bathers in black from top to toe so that the sharks could not see them, equipping them with attachments of tinkling bells to scare the monsters away, draping them with neck to knee screenings of chain. There

American John Kelly shown above and left with his controversial 'hydro' board. Kelly put a great deal of work and originality into this radical new shape. The step and the flat planing surface, with the scorpion-tail skeg, results in what its owner claims to be the fastest board afloat.

Rodney Sumpter, British and Irish and 1966 World Titles Champion.

were ideas for devices to set sirens screaming and lights blazing, walls of air bubbles dancing beneath the sea, plans for electric fences and the setting of explosive charges. Pot-shotting with rifles was suggested and the hurling of dynamite by the stick. All the ideas were carefully vetted and all of them rejected out of hand.

By mid-1937 the beaches on the Australian coast were still unprotected. It was not until someone suggested that perhaps one of the increasing numbers of overseas visitors to Australia might fall victim to a shark, thereby affording Australia a poor national advertisement, that the Government of the day offered a subsidy of $20,000 to get a shark-meshing scheme off the ground. This involved stringing fishing nets 500 feet long and twenty feet deep in series at the mouth of each bay holding a surfing beach. Using a large mesh, the nets allowed the free passage of most fish but caught the sharks by the pectoral fins or nose. The nets are examined every twenty-four hours for catches and damage. They were introduced in October 1937 and from that time until February 1939, 1,500 sharks were taken in the nets. Between 1953 and 1956 this number had fallen to 318 and between 1956 and 1959 it dropped even further to 126 and it is still dropping today to less than one a week, proving a theory that sharks like things to be easy, like to stake out their own territory, and will then attack any 'intruder'. Certainly the nets ended the shark menace, and no shark

227

fatality has been reported on any Sydney meshed beach since the nets went down for the first time.

But the shark was a passing moment of horror. The memory of it still lingers and most swimmers in the Australian surf are still aware of the shark danger, being unconvinced by the statistics that show the risk of shark attack to be infinitely smaller than the risk of death in a car accident.

The sharks could not stop the progress of

Fred Hemmings bottom turns down the face of the 'bowl' at Makaha, Hawaii.

surfing, however, and while surfers in other parts of the world were either still at the paddling stage, or concentrating on board riding as in Hawaii and California, the Australians were making techniques in their blue waters that were to have profound effects on swimming all over the world.

The major development was the emergence of the Australian crawl. At the turn of the century the fastest swimming stroke known to the world was the Trudgen style—a rather ungainly motion in which the head was lifted up and turned from side to side with each stroke, the arms hooked in the stroke and the legs making a frog-like motion. Frederick Cavill changed all that. An English immigrant to Australia in 1887, he watched the Aboriginals swimming and noticed their leg action was an up and down kick which seemed to steady their bodies in the water, producing greater speed. Cavill taught his six sons the kick and they all proved to be remarkable swimmers, particularly

An Hawaiian surfer at maximum speed beating the oncoming curl at Haleiwa, Hawaii.

Makaha surf, 1969 style—two surfers look
down from a huge wave.

Makaha, Hawaii. Tons of white water about
to fall on Greg Noll. The surf is so big
a bad wipeout would mean death.

the eldest, Richard, who became a champion
in Australia, then returned to Britain where he
assured his country of swimming supremacy
in the world for many years. Another Cavill
son, Sidney, moved to San Francisco early in
the 1900s and there taught the new stroke to
Charles Daniels who improved the stroke by
synchronizing the leg beat with the arm action
and he called it the American crawl. This stroke
was faster still and its widespread adoption in
the United States gave that country a
supremacy in world swimming that it has kept
until the present day.

The Australian crawl used by the sun-bronzed

230

Hawaii of the Sixties

Gebauer and Bob Shepherd with
own Hawaiians at Sunset Beach.

Cameramen from the American
Broadcasting Corporation shooting from
the point at Makaha for the 1964
Championships.

Local Hawaiian surfer wake-surfs in a
flooded Waikiki street from the wake of a
bus.

With a rider perched above him a surfer
finds himself in a very dangerous position
at Waimea Bay, Hawaii.

giants of the Australian surf was a delight to the
eye. Allied with their rescue and resuscitation
methods, the use of the surf reel, their
'volunteer' status, their remarkable record in
saving lives, they began attracting attention
from overseas.

Wherever swimming in the sea went on,
people were drowning, but not in Australia
when the 'volunteer' patrols were on duty.
Therefore the Australian system was worth
taking a long, hard look at. For a start, it
seemed so much more efficient than the other
organized system of sea rescue in operation—
the American system. This involved two men

231

Bobby Brown of Cronulla, New South Wales, does a difficult on-edge turn.

At fourteen Bobby Brown was showing the promise of his future success.

Fourteen-year-old Bobby Brown head dips under a small wave at Wanda Beach, New South Wales.

on shore, one of whom swam out to a swimmer in distress, taking a float to keep the patient on top of the water while the other lifesaver kept a watch and at the same time phoned for a rescue launch to call and pick up the lifesaver and patient from the water. It was certainly not a fast system, and of no use in a shark attack.

In 1934 a band of Englishmen visiting Australia watched one of the regular competitive carnivals that had become a part

of the Australian surf lifesaving movement and announced themselves tremendously impressed. They reported that there were some 2,500 deaths from drowning around the English coast in just one year. On what they had seen on the Australian beaches it was a sheer necessity, and very much a matter of life and death, that lifesaving clubs on the Australian pattern be introduced into the United Kingdom.

World War II was the factor which saw the

As if jet propelled, Bobby Brown screams down under the threatening lip of a Sandon Point, N.S.W., wall.

One of the first times Waimea was ridden, 1957. Mike Stang (top) and Mickey Munoz take a terrible wipeout.

Fred Van Dyke takes the drop at Waimea Bay, Hawaii.

Australian methods in the surf spread all over
the world. By their thousands American troops
arrived in Australia as a 'jump-off' point for
the Pacific war. They went into the seas up and
down the Australian coast, often in unpatrolled
areas, and they drowned by the dozens,
unaware of the dangers in those beautiful long
Pacific swells. In the end the American
command asked that Australian lifesavers teach
their men in the lifesaving techniques and
through the wartime period forty-three
American servicemen were awarded the Bronze
Medal of the Surf Life Saving Association for
proficiency in the surf while hundreds of
others were trained in the fundamentals giving
them a basis of knowledge that went back to
the United States with them, for development
and application on American beaches.
Australians serving in the Middle East set up
surf clubs in Egypt and Palestine. Other
troops en route to war zones got clubs going in
South Africa and Ceylon and in the years
since these clubs have prospered and been

Four of Australia's leading surfers who
competed at the Hawaiian titles in
1969—Mick Mahon, Dave Jackman,
Charlie Cardiff and Midget Farrelly.

Wally Froiseth and 'Little' John Richards
watched by Greg Noll at Sunset Beach.

Donald Takiyama really shone at Ala
Moana, 1962 'on the nose'.

Giant breakers—more than 25 feet high
offer a real challenge to even the expert
surfers at Makaha Beach, a short
distance from Honolulu. The Makaha
International Surfing Championship meet
is held at this spot each December or
January.

A beautifully executed forehand turn by skilful Australian, Bobby Brown.

Bobby Brown carves out a backhand turn at Sandon Point, New South Wales.

The classic style that won world acclaim for Bobby Brown—captured here as he stalls at Sandon Point, New South Wales.

236

joined by surf clubs in India and Hong Kong, Thailand and Singapore, Malaysia and the Philippines, on both eastern and western coasts of the African continent, in Britain and in Continental Europe, in the Channel Islands and in South America and in practically every club, the history records that it was an Australian who began the group, or that it was Australia who supplied the equipment used by the rescue patrols.

So the system of surfing for everyman, on the body, that became part of the Australian way of life and developed there of itself, spread around the world, acting as a profound influence on the way of life of millions of people. The Australians, however, were not content to brush up their rescue and resuscitation work and leave it at that. They wanted to introduce new things, new methods, to 'have a go' and the rest of the world has not yet adopted some of these innovations from Australia, particularly the surfboat or the surf ski.

Haleiwa, Makaha, Waikiki, Sunset

Surfing at Makaha—the scene of annual international surfing championships each winter. Makaha Beach on Oahu Island, provides good year-round surfing for the expert. Unskilled surfers are advised to stick to the gentler waves at Waikiki.

Once the sport of Hawaiian kings, today visitors rent boards on Waikiki Beach and tackle the tame ones, with the help of experienced instructors like this native. That's Diamond Head in the background.

The surf ski might have come about because the Australian surfers, for all their agility in the water 'on the body' illustrated no talent with the surfboards that were all the rage in Hawaii and California. The surf ski was much more manageable for the Australians, and it was invented in 1933 by Dr G. A. 'Saxon' Crackenthorp of the Manly Surf Club in Sydney. These skis vary greatly in size but average fifteen feet long by two and a half feet wide, pointed at both ends, with an upturned nose and stern joined by a gentle curve that makes them look rather like a flattened banana. They weigh around 50 pounds and are generally made of 3/16th inch marine plywood with cedar sides. The rider sits in the middle, his feet strapped in stirrups to the decking, and makes his way through the waves with a seven foot double-ended paddle. Not seen anywhere else in the world, the surf skis have proved to be of enormous use in rescues in the Australian surf, since they can be paddled out through the breaking waves

Layout of Haleiwa, from the parking spot.

Bob Pike of Australia taking a bad wipeout at Banzai Pipeline. He pulled ribs away from his spine in this roller.

Lynda Merrill and Mike Doyle doing a standing 'swan' at Makaha Championships.

Spectators watching the tandem event from Makaha Beach during the Championships.

239

A lone surfer takes off on a twenty-foot-plus wave at Waimea Bay. The geography of Waimea causes conditions like this which guarantee to separate the riders from the optimists.

Surfing at Malibu, Hawaii, in 1961. A local surfer leans his large heavy board into the glassy surf.

Bobby Brown rips across a blue wall at Sandon Point, New South Wales.

Surfing conditions in the British Isles.

Maili Beach, Hawaii—local Hawaiian surfers park their cars just off the highway to Makaha.

quickly and can act as a platform to support two, three or even four distressed patients until help can come from the shore. They are regarded as second only in usefulness in the Australian surf to the surfboat, another Australian lifesaving innovation in the way that it is manned and used, and one of the great sights of the world when they are competing against one another at an Australian surf carnival.

The benefits of having a boat available had always been obvious to the Australian lifesavers and when the 'volunteer' movement formed up and began laying down its own rules and methods, boats were high on the list of essential equipment. But what kind of boats? The early days had seen small fishing boats in use, but what was needed was a new design altogether, for a boat that was light and yet very strong, which could get out through the

In 1964, Paul Gebauer was one of the best riders at Sunset, Hawaii.

Scott Dillon, a well-known Australian board builder, drops down the face of a large wave at Sunset Beach, Hawaii.

Rusty Miller does a backhand turn at the Pipeline, Hawaii.

Paul Gebauer and Peter Cole on a bigger Sunset wave, Hawaii.

The tandem event at the Makaha Championships—two contestants show excellent control in difficult surfing.

This is a miracle in the Arizona Desert.
A wave-making machine that operates by
releasing water from a tower reservoir
through underwater gates. This creates the
wave which passes through a narrow
passage and then rushes toward the
'shore'.

Who would believe this scene is in the
Arizona Desert?

The offshore winds make Sunset very hard
to surf for these three Hawaiians.

steep, short breaking, rough Australian surf,
and get back in again without capsizing after it
had performed its rescue mission.

So the Australian surfboat, like no other boat
in the world, evolved from a kind of tuck-
sterned ship's lifeboat of heavy kauri timber, to
the shiny, varnished cedar, sleek lined, narrow
beamed racing machines of today. Every club
has one, the toughest men in the club make up
the crews, the rescue work they do is
invaluable, the spectacle of them racing
together in carnival times, unforgettable. As a
sport, it is a tough one, full of a history of
mayhem and violence, such as the fight that
became almost a riot at the Freshwater
carnival in Sydney on 25 January 1929, which
resulted in Perc Mazlin of the North Steyne
boat crew being suspended from the lifesaving
association for two years and Ralph Ford,
captain and sweep of the Manly boat, being
suspended for one year.

These surf boats are approximately twenty-two
feet in length with a five foot beam. They are

Bob Shepherd drops down a Sunset wave in Hawaii.

Walt Hoffman in trouble at Sunset.

Small Haleiwa wave—Australian surfer, 1963.

Tandem surfing in California.

One of California's best surfing areas—
Rincon Point, in very unusual conditions,
UNCROWDED.

A local surfer cutting back at the river-mouth at Santa Cruz, Northern California.

A brave surfer equipped with a safety helmet driving through the dangerous Huntington Beach piers at California.

Toes on Nose

Toes on nose—Kevin Brennen.

Typical Sunset Beach wave.

250

subject to rigid design rules, powered by a five man crew, four with one long and heavy oar each and the fifth in the stern with an even longer and heavier sweep oar.

Enormous rivalry has always been part of the boat races between the clubs and on the day of the Freshwater violence, the outstanding boat crews on the eastern Australian coast came from North Steyne and Manly clubs. Throughout a long series of carnivals, the North Steyne boat would endeavour to get ahead of the Manly boat and then would begin zig-zagging to avoid being passed. At the Freshwater carnival the Manly crew worked on a plan to allow the North Steyne boat to do its zig-zags until the turning buoy a quarter mile out to sea was reached. Then the Manly boat rammed the North Steyne boat from behind, turning it completely around. The Manly boat then went inside her rival, shot into the beach and won the race easily. When North Steyne got back to the beach Mazlin charged over to the Manly crew and began throwing punches.

Toes on nose—Judy Gibbons.

First year Australians contested in Hawaii was 1962. Here they are at Sunset Beach, Hawaii.

251

They were returned and soon about 100 brawny lifesavers were fighting like mad up and down the beach.

That near riot resulted in the lifesaving authorities ruling that the boat crews had four to six buoys to turn from instead of the one that had been the scene of so many fights. Generally the second boat at the single buoy attempted the ramming technique to push the leader out to sea so that the second boat slipped inside and when the boats came this close, all hell would break loose.

At such close quarters the rowers bow side in one boat and stroke side in the other were powerless to use their oars to propel their boats, so they pulled them from the rowlocks and use them as pushing sticks, battering rams, even bludgeons on the heads and shoulders of the rival crews.

The separated turning buoys brought an end to all that, but even today there is still intense rivalry between the boat crews and the

Layout shot of the wave conditions in the Jersey Islands.

One of Australia's best, big sea, board riders, Bob Pike, screams down the face of a big one at Waimea Bay, Hawaii. He is travelling at 25 m.p.h.

Surfers race for the start of the Welsh Surfboard Riding Championship.

The largest surf in memory hit Hawaii December, 1969. Peter Cole estimated some of the sets at over 30 feet high.

Toes on nose.

Toes on nose.

Toes on nose.

fluctuating fortunes of this boat and that, the pure excitement of those shiny long boats smashing their way out through the waves, often lifted clear of the water on their tails, and then hurtling back in again on giant waves, where one second of misjudgement results in the boat being thrown in the air and under the next wave, the boat and the heavy oars crashing down on the crew, makes for one of the most exciting spectacles in the whole spectrum of world sport. Flat bottom, high powered speedboats using the water jet principle rather than the conventional propeller drive, are now being introduced on Australian beaches, following the American practice. They are faster, can be run from the beach into the surf easily and run back out again. But it is doubtful if the man-powered surfboat will ever disappear from the Australian surf scene.

Certainly, these boats appear old-fashioned. But there is much of this old-fashioned

Toes on nose.

Here is a sight not often seen—a beautiful set of waves pouring in round the Cornish coast and not a surfer in sight.

'Sunset' Africa—South Africa's answer to Hawaii's famed Sunset Beach. Local surfers often ride twenty foot waves at this spot.

approach and attitude bound up in the history and tradition of the Australian surfing movement. And nothing more old fashioned that the now-all-but-dead controversy on just what the Australian surf bather is allowed to wear on his own beaches.

The controversy over the wearing of 'neck-to-knee' costumes that followed the fuss over daylight bathing might have seemed to end in favour of the surfers. But officialdom doesn't let go as easily as that. Nearly twenty years after the original insistence by the authorities that surf bathers should cover their bodies from the public gaze, the New South Wales Government in March 1921, promulgated the following new regulation:

'All persons over four years of age bathing in any waters exposed to the public view other than baths . . . shall be clad in a bathing costume covering the body from the neck to the knee so as to secure the observance of decency; and any inspector may require any person contravening this provision to resume

Wayne Williams, Newcastle Beach, New South Wales. Superb control by an aggressive surfer.

at once his ordinary dress.'
Any swimmer not conforming to this regulation 'may with any necessary force, be removed to the dressing shed or enclosure by the inspector'. The regulations were made to look the more insane by the next paragraph which set out that in public baths all persons above the age of eight years had to be in neck-to-knees, leaving the tots from four years of age to eight in a no-man's land of nudity. The regulations were laughed at, of course, but they were followed at first and only the passage of the years and the designs of the swimsuit makers slowly whittled away the cloth to expose more and more Australian flesh to the sun. But the final ridiculous situation arose in 1936 when, following a number of cases of bathers being ordered from beaches because of their dress, the Surf Lifesaving Association wrote to Mr Eric Spooner, the New South Wales Minister of Works and Local Government, asking him to allow shorts for men on the beaches.

Toes on nose—Garry Birdsall.

The S.L.S.A. reported that road workers stripped to the waist on the job, boxers and wrestlers were stripped to the waist in public performances, the movies were full of men with naked chests, yet no ditch digger ran any risk of prosecution on the grounds he had upset decency. What is more, the association pointed out, shorts were more efficient in the surf and made for better lifesaving. After all, the King of England wore shorts when he bathed in public, would he be prosecuted for wearing

Toes on nose—Bob Brown.

Toes on nose at Greenmount, Queensland, 1966.

Toes on nose.

Toes on nose—Kevin Parkinson.

259

Toes on nose—Bobby Brown, 1966.

The rugged Spanish coastline presents hazards to surfers at popular San Sebastian. Note the heavy, uneven surf.

Layout shot of Cat Bay, Phillip Island, Victoria—one of Australia's most popular surfing areas.

Toes on nose.

Toes on nose—Frank Latta, North Werri, N.S.W.

the same attire when he visited Australia? A most reasonable case, yet Minister Spooner gave a flat no. He had just introduced a new ordinance up-dating the neck to knee regulation, but the new ordinance required the chest of all bathers to be covered from armpits downwards to avoid 'the brassiere costume causing offence to other members of the public'. What is more, he told the S.L.S.A., he had received a letter from the good matron ladies of the Country Women's Association in Bega, a small hamlet on the far and lone South Coast of New South Wales, which he quoted: 'The conduct of the male bathers at our two principal swimming places of the district, namely Tathra Beach and the junction of the Bega and Brogo Rivers, in lowering their costumes so as to form trunks, is, in the opinion of our branch, disgusting and merits vigorous attention.'

But this Alice in Wonderland situation was prevented from going too far. The local councils supervising the surfing beaches in

New South Wales did not enforce the new regulations and the bathers didn't wait for Spooner to change his mind, they got into their trunks and moved into the world, at least as far as beach attire was concerned.

There were other ways in the world of surfing, in which Australia was far, far behind. She had developed surfing her own way, providing influences that were to affect surfing around the world. Through all this development Australia had barely been touched by the other major surfing influence, that of Hawaii

261

Toes on nose.

Toes on nose—Phil Parkinson.

and California, the influence of board riding in the surf.

The resurgence of board riding in Hawaii began to spill over into the rest of the world with the emergence of Duke Kahanamoku, the lithe 'human fish' from Hawaii, the world's champion swimmer. He won the 100 metres swim events at the 1912 and 1920 Olympic Games and restored to the Hawaiians their long lost pride in water sports. But his wins did more than that. The Duke's powerful swimming style in which he used to appear to glide across the top of the water rather than thrash through it, focussed the world's attention on Hawaii. In 1920 the American swimming team at the Olympic Games included seven Hawaiians and Warren Kealoha and later 'Buster' Crabbe and Bill Smith succeeded Kahanamoku as winners of the Olympic Games swim sprints.

Travel writers began making the journey to Hawaii to write of the Hawaiians and their skill in the water. Unaware that in Australia men and women by the thousands were quickly mastering the art of body surfing, the visiting Caucasians watched the Hawaiians in the water and wrote determinedly that this was an occupation only the islanders could do, no white man could ever hope to emulate them. But that is not the way of man. Faced with the surf as a perpetual challenge, what is another one, except to be mastered?

Toes on nose—Kevin Parkinson.

Toes on nose.

Toes on nose—Kevin Parkinson.

So it was that George Freeth, the Hawaiian, was taken on his exhibitions on the Californian Coast by the Pacific Electric Railroad company, thus giving board riding and surfing its start in California. It very quickly caught on and Duke Kahanamoku himself followed Freeth to California to give the new sport another fillip. In 1915 the Duke was also invited to Australia to compete against the Australian champions in pool meets. The Duke took his first look at the Sydney beaches and could not understand why there were no board riders on those long, hollow waves. He was told that a board had been brought into Australia by C. D. Paterson in 1912. It was a Hawaiian board, a solid,

Hanging five, a local surfer strives to beat
the wave at Sandon Point, N.S.W.

The Best Places

Toes on nose at Currumbin Beach,
Queensland.

heavy, redwood slab which nobody could manage in the rougher surfs of Australia— mainly because all the would-be riders attempted to use the board in the shallow, broken waves close to shore, not understanding that the pressure of deep water was required beneath the board to give balance and mobility.

Paterson's board had been tossed aside unused for three years. Nobody mentioned it to Duke Kahanamoku when he spoke of boards, everyone had forgotten those early disastrous attempts to emulate the mastery of the Hawaiians. So the Duke went to a Sydney timber firm, got himself a length of sugar pine and carved out his own board. He took it down to Freshwater Beach and turned on a blinding display of turns, slides, kick-offs and runs diagonally along the face of the waves. He did it all with such astonishing ease that he had the crowd watching totally enthralled. That day Freshwater made the Duke a King and the

A spot named the 'Pass' at Byron Bay, North Coast, N.S.W.

Beautiful top to bottom wave typical of North Narrabeen, N.S.W.

265

Scott's Head, N.S.W., showing the beautiful fast, hollow take-off which wraps around the point to disappear along the beachfront for a very long, fast ride.

board he used still stands in the Freshwater Club.

In the crowd that day was a youngster named Claude West. What the Duke was doing with his sugar pine board absolutely entranced West and he approached the Duke afterwards and asked to be the master's pupil. Kahanamoku gave West the sugar pine board and hours of instruction. West was a good pupil and the most outstanding of all the riders who emerged with their boards as a result of the Duke's Freshwater display. That one day began board riding in Australia with a bang, and board races quickly became part of the regular surfing carnivals. The first Australian surfboard championships were held soon after World War I and the winner was Claude West.

After that introduction, however, board riding in Australia remained rather stagnant. All the development was going on in California which was fast becoming the world's surfing centre. Hawaii might have been and might yet remain the Mecca for surfers of the world, but

John Cunningham of Queensland making a nice wave at Kirra, Queensland.

The dangerous take-off area at Bare Island, Sydney.

Beautiful Kirra wave in Queensland flowing 'inside out'.

Crowded conditions at Port Hacking Bay, Sydney, as board riders fight for positions.

At Voodoo Bay, near Kurnell, Sydney, a surfer shields his face from the setting sun to see his way clear out of the wave.

Laurie Shorts drives hard along a wave at Nullarbor Plain, West Australia.

California in those early days and right through to the present time, was the world's surfing workshop, the design centre, the origin of all the major developments in the sport.

The first major development came from thought the young Californian surfers gave to the Hawaiian boards they were using. They checked the Hawaiian history and found that the weight of the Hawaiian board was related to the wealth and power of the man who rode it, apart from the fact that the board needed to be substantial to take the weight of the massively built islanders who weighed up to 20 stone. The Californians neither ate nor weighed so much as the early Hawaiians and had other prestige symbols. They didn't need heavy boards to show how much money they had. So began the search for lightness. In the late 1920's California's Tom Blake designed and built a hollow board that was quite fast and paddled easily and with it he won most of the surfing and paddling events he entered.

Those early Blake boards weighed around 100 pounds, but design improvement got them down to 60 pounds fairly quickly. They were long, narrow boards and they and the solid pine and redwood boards of Hawaii set the pattern of world surfing in the years prior to World War II. Yet their popularity was not great. They were too heavy and cumbersome out of the water in a day and age when the automobile was a luxury owned by very few. Obviously, to popularize surfing, the boards had to be made lighter, more portable, more easily paddled. Balsa boards were tried, more hollow centres were tried. The great Californian surfer Preston 'Pete' Peterson, built a pair of all-balsa boards in the 1930s but the wood was too soft, causing the protective coating of varnish to crack easily, after which the balsa became waterlogged and rotten. But the idea was sound and the later discovery of fibreglass cloth and plastic resins to laminate the glass to the wood saw the birth of the modern surfboard and a limitless future for the sport.

But fibreglass and plastic resin were unknown to the pioneers. Tom Blake, who had been the swimming champion of the world between the reigns of Duke Kahanamoku and Johnny Weismuller, was the design leader with his hollow boards that went so fast. In 1928 Blake presented a cup for the United States Pacific Coast surfing championship and won it himself, easily. In 1930 he moved to Hawaii to take on the traditional champions, using a 16 foot long redwood board, pointed at both ends like a

Through the 'Pass' at Byron Bay, N.S.W., a local surfer shows his back on an unusual angle.

Kennett River, Victoria, a favourite surfing spot.

cigar and only 16 inches wide. The Hawaiians hadn't seen such a board before, their races had always been won with maximum 12 foot boards with wide bows and tails. But Blake's board was allowed and he commenced to re-write the record book. The Hawaiians were chagrined and made a few inquiries which resulted in their discovering that Blake's board was HOLLOW. There was uproar but Blake fought it out and had his board approved, which removed any limit on the size and

Huge wave explodes behind Kerry Butcher at Shell Harbour breakwater.

270

With the concrete breakwater as a backdrop, Ken Middleton hangs five at Shell Harbour.

Local South-side surfer surfing the ground
swells at Port Hacking Bay, Sydney.

shape of surfboards that could be used in
competitions.

The boards immediately grew to vast sizes.
Long timbers 24 feet from bow to stern and
only 16 inches wide appeared in the waves and
the men who paddled them had to be big
and strong to move them at all. But once they
moved they developed enormous momentum,
with a long, free-wheeling glide. Hawaiian
greats such as Tom Kiakona, Sam Reid, Jack
May and Same and Duke Kahanamoku got
themselves Blake style boards and set to
paddling like whirlwinds. Once again the
surfers were back in the place of Kings on
Oahu. The men who surfed at Waikiki on
those long gentle swells found again Makaha
and Sunset Beach and Waimea Bay on the
north side of the island where the huge swells
from Arctic storms decanted onto the shallow
coral reefs. The big boards could handle these
big surfs and suddenly, in the 1930s, spots
that had not been surfed for centuries all
around Hawaii were ringing again with the

Kevy Parkinson, Shell Harbour, showing the spot where water comes through under the breakwater.

Piha Beach, New Zealand—with two large headlands in centre known as the 'Camels', and at lower right of these, are two small rocks known as the 'Beehive'. Photo was taken during heavy off-shore breeze, which allows no heavy surf.

Port Kembla, N.S.W.

Werri Beach, South Coast, N.S.W., surfers in a contest, watched by a dog.

Hawaiian equivalent of 'out the back'. In California the hollow board was being widely used for both surfing and paddling and more personalities were emerging to give the new sport a push along. The famed Gene 'Tarzan' Smith was one of these, indeed, he was undoubtedly the greatest marathon paddler of all time. He came from Balboa, California, and went to Hawaii in 1936 to compete in paddling races and to set himself endurance tests. He would often paddle his board several miles out to sea from Waikiki beach, out of sight over the horizon, just for an afternoon's fun. In 1938 he paddled from the island of Molokai to Makapua, Oahu, in

272

Tight in the tube at Angourie, North Coast, N.S.W., a surfer drives hard to make the wave to beat a bad wipeout on the rocks in the foreground.

eight hours fifteen minutes, a distance of about twenty-six miles.

But that was only a training spin. At 3.45 p.m. on 14 October 1940, he left Kaena Point, Oahu, on his 13 foot, 90 pound board and almost reached Koloa, Kauai, on the following day, covering more than seventy miles in thirty hours in heavy seas. He was severely stung by a Portuguese man-o'-war on the way and was once confronted by a giant, twelve foot wide manta ray that had to be shot by an attendant on an accompanying guard boat before Smith could paddle on.

But not every surfer was a Tarzan Smith or a Tom Blake. For most, the big paddle boards remained too unwieldy, too heavy, until the experiments began with balsa boards. One of the great pioneers in this field was 'the man with the withered arm' Bob Simmons. A student at the California Institute of Technology, Simmons was considered to have a brilliant future ahead of him, until he was involved in a motor cycle accident and so badly mangled his arm he was told he had to constantly exercise it or it would have to be amputated. Even so, the arm was withered and lacked strength. But in the hospital receiving treatment, Simmons became interested in surfing by a fellow patient and went looking for the water on his discharge. From 1934 on,

Late waves at Crescent Head pour into the
bay as two surfers catch different waves.

Inside a tight wave at Kirra, Queensland.

Long lines of swells from Bass Strait wrap
around Cat Bay, Phillip Island, Victoria.

Grabbing the rail of his board to maintain balance, a surfer crouches at Kirra Beach, Queensland.

Simmons roamed the California coast living on cottage cheese and canned peaches and crusts of bread, watching the waves, shaping surfboards, becoming steeped in the surfing lore.

He developed an enormous dislike for the surfboards of the day, those long 100 pound monsters he found impossible to carry with his bad arm, and yet he had to have a board, had to ride one, to manage one. So he began experimenting with first the balsa boards and varnish and then fibreglass and after that, the polyfoam boards that made the real breakthrough in surfboard design.

In his backyard in Pasadena, Simmons used his university training to study flow dynamics in the relationship between a surfboard and a wave and on the results he achieved, worked on the design of a new style board. He was the first to shape the top as well as the bottom of a board. He put a real turn-up on the nose, improving the board's performance, balance and appearance in one act. Simmons was always working for improvements, always theorizing on where he might find the best and biggest surf to ride. Surf was his love, and as it happened, his death. In September 1954 he disappeared while riding a big surf at La Jolla, California. His body was washed up a few days later. No one saw what happened

The Bells Beach contest in Victoria, with the judges watching a contestant take off on one of the beautiful big swells.

to him, the theory is that he was hit by his own board, knocked unconscious and drowned. The debt today's surfers owe to Simmons is an enormous one. His designs, his light boards, had all the desired advantages. They could be carried by the average man or woman since they weighed as little as 25 pounds. They could be paddled easily and were very buoyant, which allowed them to come in quite small sizes in comparison with the previous redwood planks. The small size allowed for greater

manoeuvrability, making the present 'hot dogging' style of surfing possible. Surfing stunts and styles such as walking the nose, hanging five or ten, fast turns and pullouts and fast takeoffs became possible. These light, Simmons style boards were first made popular on the surfing beach at Malibu, and so became known as Malibu boards.

The next boost that was to change the style of board surfing and spread it in a boom all over the world, was the developments made in the technology of plastics. Polyurethane foam boards could be moulded, colours could be added to the laminating resins. One surfer even had a colour photograph of a painting of a Roman Bacchanal moulded under the fibreglass cover of his board, and he named the board The Orgy. With these type boards, semi-mass production—impossible with hand shaped balsa—became possible.

Matt Kivlin of Santa Monica, California, was another of the pioneers to change the shape and style of boards and popularize the sport.

A very rugged piece of South African shoreline and a challenging surfing scene.

Big 12 foot waves pour around Terrigal Haven, N.S.W., off the point, nearly wiping out the cameraman.

277

Burleigh Heads, Queensland, off the point is a surfer flying along the first break to beat the rocks in the foreground.

The opening to the 'Farm', Bass Point, N.S.W.—A place 'discovered' by South Coast surfers in 1962.

He was one of the first to produce surfboards commercially, and would sit on the beach at Santa Monica carving out balsa until the wind-blown shavings created a public nuisance. So he rented a shop, and the modern, one-man custom surfboard factory was born. He was one of the first to use polyurethane foam and some of his boards were the first on Malibu when the then surfing stars such as Buzzy Trent, Peter Cole and Tom Zahn had begun their surfing careers. Peter Lawford, the actor, was also a regular and in 1954 Lawford travelled to Australia on film work and took a Malibu board with him. It was the first such board to be seen 'Down Under' and indeed, few people took any notice of it. Nobody had heard of the Californian revolution that was putting a surfboard at the disposal of every surfer, that was opening up totally new surfing horizons. Nobody became aware that the Californian surfers on their light ply boards were learning tricks and manoeuvres in minutes that the 'oldies' had taken years to master on the heavy

Beautiful surf at Crescent Head, N.S.W.

The layout of the 'Farm', Bass Point, N.S.W., can be seen here as a set breaks in the centre of the beach.

Scott Dillon locked in on a big wave at Narrabeen, N.S.W., while surfers on the front wave remain unaware of what's behind them.

Young local surfer locked in at Kirra, Queensland. The beach is famous for these beautifully-shaped waves.

planks that were still in use generally in Australia.

World War II had a profound effect on the history of surfing. It broke down the communication barrier that had caused Australian surfing to develop almost in its own vacuum, and it allowed to simmer the changes that were taking place in board riding, so that they boiled over rapidly at war's end and spread throughout the world. Australians posted overseas taught their lifesaving methods and particularly made the Americans aware of the Australian surfing system. So interested were they, that in 1956 the United States Government sponsored a group of top surfers on a trip to Australia to coincide with the Melbourne Olympic Games. The group was led by the redoubtable Tom Zahn. The Americans brought their Malibu boards with them and gave exhibitions at surf carnivals up and down the eastern Australian coast. The effect on the Australian surfer was even more dramatic than the exhibition given by

Danny Keyo inside a well-shaped wave at North Narrabeen, N.S.W.

Fred Farmer head dips under a beach wave at Cronulla Beach, N.S.W.

Kevin Parkinson in trouble at the Bellambi Pier, N.S.W.

Duke Kahanamoku at Freshwater had been forty years before. Every Australian surfer who watched the Americans simply had to have a Malibu board. Which wasn't easy since balsa was then unobtainable in Australia, but within weeks the first plywood copies of the boards Zahn's team used were in the water, urgent enquiries were being made of the board builders in California and the first Australian board manufacturers were tooling up for business. By 1959 the boardmakers were producing 1,500 Malibu boards a year, a figure that had grown five times by 1962 and the same rate of increase has persisted until the present day.

So the Americans took the Hawaiian Sport of Kings and developed it and spread it across the Pacific to start a surfing revolution. They found good disciples in the Australians who travelled to Europe and to South Africa, to Hong Kong and Ceylon, to Britain and the Channel Isles, spreading the gospel of the

Barry 'Chubby' Kirkham, performs a classical bottom-turn on beautiful glassy water at Oak Park, Sydney.

Malibu board wherever they went, introducing the sport in those countries.

And once surfing spread, of course, it had to be naturally decided who was the best at it. While World War II had broken the surfing communications barrier, it had also brought active surfing to a standstill. When the war ended, a new generation of surfers stepped in and took over the scene, the youngsters, the new breed. In 1947 the Waikiki Surf Club was started to look after the young swimmers.

Phillip Island, Victoria, famous as the nesting home for penguins, is another popular surfing spot.

Long lines of swell wrap around the point at Greenmount, Coolangatta, Queensland.

Local surfer inside a tight wall at Windang Island, South Coast, N.S.W.

Near Kempsey, N.S.W.

283

Keith Paul

Beautiful tight surfing by Keith Paul as he uses the critical part of this wave for greater speed and control. A skilful surfer, Keith won the 1968 Australian Titles defeating both Nat Young and Midget Farrelly.

Running along the top of the wave Keith Paul re-enters into smooth water.

Rental boards and instructors began to appear to give the tourists a real taste of Hawaii; on a summer's day you couldn't move on the waters of Waikiki Beach for board riders. It was the same story in California. From the handful of devotees who once surfed Malibu, the beach crowd had grown to impossible proportions. Board makers opened up for business on every corner, from a few hundred pre-war surfers the crowds shot up to more than a quarter million on the West Coast alone. With so much interest, with the formation of clubs, there just had to be competition.

So in 1954 the first International Championships were held at Makaha, Hawaii. In that year George Downing, the famous coach of the Outrigger Canoe Club, won the senior men's division to be regarded as top surfer in the world. Points were awarded on length of ride, number of waves caught, grace, skill and sportsmanship. Rabbit Kekai, Conrad Cunha, Jamma Kekai, Peter Cole, Wally Froiseth, Buffalo Keaulana and again George Downing in 1962, were subsequent titleholders, so that by far the highest proportion of champions were Hawaiian-born. But Hawaii's two main rivals for world surfing supremacy were catching up fast. The Americans had been running competitions since the 1930s at the San Onofre Surfing Club of California and the movement had spread to the United States east coast with the first East Coast Surfing Championships being held at Daytona Beach, Florida, on Labour Day, 1939.

Keith Paul made this wave with the curl hitting right along to the shoulder.

A head dip while making a hand rail turn in the Australian Championships at Long Reef, N.S.W. Keith Paul really turns it on to take out the title.

Again the very tight surfing style can be seen as Paul grabs the rail for more balance.

The Surfing Movie People

Australian movie maker, Bob Evans (left), produced some excellent footage which helped put Australia on the international surfing scene.

In Australia, the Malibu riders formed themselves into an association and began running their own contests, competitions were going on in New Zealand and South Africa, surfing magazines were popping up by the score, surfing movies were doing smash business in the cinemas, the sport had really taken off, to the point where the first World Surfing Championships were organized, with entrants from Australia, California and Hawaii. The surprise was that these championships were not to be held in the traditional home of surfing—Hawaii—but in Australia. The year was 1963 and the winner of the contest was an Australian, Bernard 'Midget' Farrelly. The second world championship contest was held in Peru and was won by the Peruvian Felipe Pomar, the third series in San Diego, California was won by an Australian again in Robert 'Nat' Young who lost the title in the next championship meet at Rincon, Puerto Rico to the Hawaiian Fred Hemmings. But it was a close thing, the final placings in that 1968 championship going to Hemmings by two points (364) to Australia's Farrelly (362) followed by Russell Hughes of Australia, Nat Young of Australia, Mike Doyle of California and in sixth place Reno Abellero of Hawaii. The Australians had been slow to catch up with the world of the Malibu board, but once near the top, they began setting a hot pace.

The world championships, the American national championships, the international meets in Mexico, Peru and in France where screen writer Peter Viertel had introduced a Malibu board and the sport in 1956, the Makaha

286

Big 'Gun' of the movie world. Television cameras filming the 1969 World Titles.

American Bud Brown produced the first movie of surf riding the big waves at Sunset and Makaha. Is still regarded as one of the best.

Cameramen setting up their equipment to photograph a surfing contest. Interest in 1966 was high, partly due to the outstanding performances of Australians Nat Young and Midget Farrelly.

International and the Duke Kahanamoku contests in Hawaii, established a 'jet set' of surfers from all parts of the world, cementing the sport and spreading its influence wider and deeper throughout the globe. By the end of the '60s there were strong surfing movements in Israel, England, Canada, Ceylon, India, West Africa, North Africa, Chile, Brazil, Formosa, Malaya and Thailand as well as the strongholds of the United States, Hawaii, Australia, South Africa and New Zealand.

All over the world, the youngsters with their boards and their sun-bleached hair, their somewhat outlandish clothes, their 'surfari' wagons with half a dozen boards on top, hunting the waves up and down miles of coastline, were a familiar sight as they pursued 'a way of life, one we surfers would not swap for any other, this remarkable intoxication of speeding down waves with that incredible, roaring, rushing, zipping sound beneath you, pulse racing, knees jiggling, head in the salt-tanged air'.

The Sport of Kings had gone to the common man. From the days before Captain Cook when the Polynesian islanders had taken their tree trunks and planks out into the surf to find their fun and found their culture, surfing had become a major international sport, big business, the recreation of millions.

Up to the 19th century those early surfers had been content to lie on their boards, paddle out into the surf, catch a wave, perhaps stand up and then speed straight ahead in one

Bruce Brown, producer of *Endless Summer, Surfing, Hollow Days, Bare Foot Adventure*, and *Slippery When Wet*, is probably the biggest and most successful movie maker on the surfing scene.

The other surf shooting equipment.

Kevin Brennen

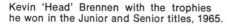
Kevin 'Head' Brennen with the trophies he won in the Junior and Senior titles, 1965.

direction. Today, with their new boards and modern imaginations, the young surfers of the world have wreaked their changes. Now every new wave is a challenge, and today's experienced surfer plays the wave as he rides it—speeding up, slowing down, turning, swerving, changing direction, riding in the trough, shooting along the crest. He can turn to the left by placing his foot on the board's right edge and leaning in that direction. He can stall by stepping back on the board or speed forward by 'walking the nose'. Like a young boy taunting a policeman a surfer tempts the edge of rolling water until it nearly devours him, then with quick footwork and fine balancing, the board shoots across the watery wall, momentarily out of danger, until the gleeful surfer cuts deftly back to tempt fate again.

As surfing authority Peter L. Dixon once described it: 'Surfing is a challenge requiring intense concentration. The total range of senses is engaged in keeping the body in balance and the wave from dominating the rider. This is particularly true in big surf. On smaller, well-formed waves there is time to look around, to wave to a friend and plan ahead. But the surfer who lets his attention lag will lose to the wave. Waves are living, moving things and no two waves are alike. This infinite variety gives surfing colour, excitement, action. Yet surfing is uncomplicated. In the frightfully complex world of modern technology nothing is quite as refreshingly simple as a functional surfboard and waves, sun and sky.'

On a wave at North Avalon, Kevin 'Head' Brennen 'bicycles' through the inside section.

The 'Head' on the nose in the Australian Junior titles, 1964.

A very young Kevin Brennen about to enter the water at North Avalon, N.S.W., 1962.

Perfect control as he 'hangs ten' in a contest between Northside and Wind 'n' Sea, 1966.

California

Ricky Hatch trims in the white water at Hermosa Beach, California.

Very cold conditions in San Francisco make skin suits a must—with a backdrop of mountains and offshore winds, three surfers brave the elements to ride this good surf.

Unidentified surfer speeding on to the shorebreak at San Onofre on a long board.

Jackson Snider finds a wave to himself at Malibu Beach, California.

'Surfing is uncomplicated,' says Dixon. Yes it is, and no it is not. The early Hawaiians bound their surfing up with their religious beliefs and their society. Early Hawaiian surfing was closely interwoven with mysticism. Then it became a sport and—by the late '60s—the mysticism was making a return. For thousands of the young men of the world surfing became a way of life, with its own gods, the sun and the wave, with its own rules, its own community life. Or perhaps it is a non-community life.

The two major influences on surfing as a sport, the Australian surf lifesaving movement and the introduction of the Malibu board, are in reality two opposite forces. They met head on in Australia.

The surf lifesaving movement, being a volunteer body intent on saving people's lives, is very much a 'community' effort, its very being is essentially 'mateship', comradeship, the togetherness of clubs, the combined effort. Board riding to growing numbers of young people, is directly the opposite. As former world champion Nat Young tells it: 'Surfing is finding yourself. There's no room for clubs. The sport is too individual. There have been many attempts at forming surfers organizations but they don't really work. When you start organizing surfing, everybody peels off. Riding waves is a very personal thing, it's a sport for egomaniacs and in that way it is not what traditional society would call healthy. The surfrider is far too involved in himself to the exclusion of all others. What the individual creates is the "in" thing.'

Malibu, 1961, part of the scene with surfers waiting for some of the crowded surfers to come in—note the shapes and sizes of boards.

Local Malibu surfer sits high on a good wave at Malibu, 1961.

That point of view, or philosophy, if you like, has caused problems in the past and will cause more in the future. The beaches of the world are becoming increasingly crowded. If increasing numbers of surfriders insist on 'doing their own thing' on these beaches and ignoring the comfort of their fellows— particularly the non-riders—clashes are inevitable. In California and in Australia the beaches have already been split up into sections for boardriders and sections for swimmers, forming two communities with different ideas, different approaches towards surfing. The outcome of this schizophrenic situation yet remains to be seen.

One of the greatest problems that has faced surfing is its search for respectability. Throughout the growth years from the late 1950s through to the early 1960s, the board rider was considered to be 'low class' or, as the Americans describe them, bums. They were looked down on by the body surfers of

Unique layout shot of Malibu, 1961—
showing the crowded conditions and
perfect shape of the swell as it lines round
the point.

David Nuuhiwa crouches inside a tight
curl at Huntington Beach, California.

Australia, regarded as vagabonds when they
went wandering around the world looking for
waves; in the United States they were banned
from many areas and despised in most others.
In Australia two factions flared and fought for
a brief period—the 'rockers' and the 'surfies'.
The rockers were young men from inland
Sydney suburbs who seldom visited the beaches
for recreation, preferring to take to the roads
on motor bikes and 'hot' cars. They despised
the sun bleached, healthy looking young

295

A surfer with safety helmet, at the Huntington Beach contest, tearing through a long wall.

Jim Blears, from Hawaii, rips into a re-entry at the Huntington Beach contest.

surfers who seemed to be able to win the hearts of all the girls, and several near-riots and many an ugly scene took place at the beaches when the rockers arrived in their motorized armies to taunt and battle with the surfers. The resultant publicity did the surfers no good at all in their search for a better image. The basis of the problem was, and still is, that surfing on boards has been adopted throughout the world as the sport of the young man, the boy becoming a man, full of all the rebellious instincts, the search for personal identity that is in every healthy young boy in any part of the world. Shaking off the disciplines of the family nest, spreading their wings into their 'own life' the young surfers had this desire for freedom well fed by the waves and the sun and the exhilaration of screaming down a good wave. They had no intention of giving that up without a big fight. And fights there were. On the increasingly crowded beaches parents watched anxiously as their children, happily

Dru Harrison sits on half his board after it hit one of the pilings, the front half of the board floats ahead.

The piers confront Reno Abellero as he fights to control his board.

body surfing or paddling were being threatened with sudden death by out-of-control boards. Several deaths and many injuries were sustained from flying boards while the board riders ran amok among the non-board riders. Beach authorities, local government officials and the community at large set up an outcry that again further alienated the board rider, and when it was decided all over the world, to divide the beaches in many areas with one section for swimmers—the main part of the

A surfer about to enter between the piers
in the Huntington Beach contest.

beach, and the fringes for the boards, the
alienation became segregation.

Up to the 1970s there was little contact between
the two groups. In Australia and the United
States attempts were made to organize the
board riders into clubs with rules and some
possible hope of introducing a 'community'
spirit that would improve the surfers' image
and end the 'segregation'. Such efforts met with
little success. Many young men were attracted
to surfing because of the 'mod' image and not
because of the skills required. An old car and
a board on top and a young man was suddenly
a surfer whether he was likely to drown in the
water or not. So they got their full recognition
in other ways, by using rough language,
destroying property in acts of hooliganism and

vandalism and so the image of the surfer
was further downgraded.

In the United States where surfboard riding
was extremely popular the problem became
most acute. One by one beaches were shut
down to board riders, segregated, or the surfers
given set hours when they could ride, the hour
often coinciding with a flat sea. Surfing movies
were banned in many places in the States
because of disorderly crowds, near riots and
general destruction. In San Diego and Newport,
almost every auditorium and school at one
time closed its doors to the popular surfing
films. In an attempt to halt the sliding image
of the surfer, the more responsible among them
formed the United States Surfing Association
to cope with the many problems of the growing

Large crowds on the pier watch a contestant at Huntington Beach during the annual contest.

This could be the surfer's answer to the high-kick.

The acceleration at Cronulla Point proves too much for this surfer as he heads for a bad wipeout.

sport. The top surfers, the surfboard makers, the film makers and the beach lifeguards got together and after a creaky start began making headway. They faced the same problem that has faced surfing organizations all over the world, in that they too were dealing with 'loners' who only wanted to know what the organization could do for them, not what they could do for the organization and the sport in general.

But the U.S. Surfing Association pressed on, meeting with beach councils and playing the political game. They saved many beaches from closure to board riders and then opened their own beach exclusively for Association members. Other clubs started up using the Association as a model and a parent body and gradually some pride of a kind other than in their own prowess began to grow in the surfing ranks. It was a difficult task. In Australia attempts to start clubs for board riders were marked with either failure or indifferent success—for the Australian character, the individualism and

A hazardous wipeout.

scorn for authority which gave bathing in the sea at Manly its start at the end of the last century was again strong in Australian youth. Still he scorns authority, yet is intelligent enough to believe he can make a better world by his own efforts, forsaking assistance from outside. He is a 'loner' in every sense. He resists all efforts to be organized into groups for the betterment of the sport. He scorns the 'oldies', the veteran surfers who have had a background of the surf lifesaving clubs and

Playing it Safe

'I am the greatest'.

This is my 'toes over'.

'This is how I wave to my fans'. 'Hello fans'.

This is my forehand turn—notice my style.

The crowds and the confusion on the main surfing beaches of the world and the 'loner' philosophy of the rider have had one healthy effect—they have pushed the surfriders out into the world in search of new waves in less crowded locations. Increasing numbers of the top surfers of the world spend half their years in their home surfs and the other half on world wide surfaris, taking in the waves of Hawaii and Peru, Morocco and Portugal, France and Mexico, Australia and South Africa in one long endless summer of waves and salt air and challenges, challenges, challenges.

Hawaii is the surfer's paradise, their Mecca. It seems made by Nature specifically for surfing. It has a general coastal water temperature of 70 degrees Fahrenheit, it has coral reefs to shape the swells into waves and a fortunate location, in that it is in the path of the Pacific's dominant swells. Oahu, the island most suited for surfing, receives ground swells from both the North and South Pacific—the north swell in October-January as it rolls away from the winter storms near Siberia and Alaska, and from June to October the southern swells from the winter storms in the Antarctic. Add

who believe the same organization can be set up for board riders, or better still, the two interests combined. Such 'oldies' do not understand modern surfing, the 'loners' claim and so they retreat further into their segregation. In their minds is but one thought, to escape from all the agitation and the turmoil and the crowds, and find waves to ride. And they hold the serious belief that riding waves is the only thing for them in life and the only thing that will ever be. Such is the charm and innocence of the young.

Local North Avalon surfer rips into a rail-turn.

to this the bonus of Hawaii's own seasonal typhoons and hurricanes and you have surfing all the year round, in great variety to suit every level of riding skill.

For beginners there are the gentle little rollers of Waikiki, for the professionals the terrifying twenty-five foot giants of Makaha and Sunset Beach—waves that can snap a board or a back like a twig. And there is the Banzai Pipeline. Discovered in the winter of 1961-2, the Pipeline is without doubt the most exciting surfing spot

Spectacular Rides

in the world and without doubt one of the most dangerous. Picture a ten foot wave coming out of a twenty foot depth of water and suddenly hitting a rock reef only six feet below the surface.

The wave mounts in the air and then collapses as a brick wall would collapse, causing a tube or pipe in the face of every wave. A surfer with experience can ride them but he still has no assurance that he will not spear head-first into the rocky bottom. The Pipeline is located

between Waimea Bay and Sunset Beach and is rideable up to eight or ten feet on the inside reef, moving out as the surf increases in size. The outside wave, although bigger, is actually a safer ride but the surfer may find himself locked in and the victim of the crushing shorebreak. There is no convenient channel to paddle out through but rather a roaring current that can sweep the surfer half a mile up the beach in a matter of minutes. The current in a way is a blessing, for it has dissuaded a good

Though the nose of his board had been ripped off on the rocks, Mick Brown shows beautiful control as he trims through a big wave.

Body surfers dive out of the way as Bill Penrue (inside) and Brian Jackson drive along the wall.

many surfers from trying their luck on the Banzai Pipeline.

In California, the most popular surfing spots range from Kelly's Cove in San Francisco to the Tjuana Sloughs on Imperial Beach at the Mexican border. Scattered between these two locations are hundreds of excellent board riding areas—some of them among the best in the world. California's western exposure offers swells from the year-round storms of the Pacific and the storm swells sweep in from many

miles out, smoothing themselves on the long
journey into long, even lines. The waves are
generally not big, reaching ten to twelve feet
in the summer and slightly taller in the winter.
In most areas in California the best surfing is
from October to January, the coldest time of
the year with water temperatures down to 50
degrees Fahrenheit in some areas, making the
neoprene rubber surf jacket an essential. The
major surf areas in the state are the San
Francisco - Santa Cruz area, Santa Barbara -

Ventura, the Malibu-South Bay-Palos Verdes section, the Orange County area and the Oceanside to the Mexican Border section.

In recent years the major interest in surfing has switched from the United States West Coast to the East. There are now more active surfers on the East Coast than on the West and the surfing is organized to an almost 'professional' stage, not unlike the circuits of the professional golfers, with regular contests and public appearances before good crowds paying money at the 'gate' at surfing centres stretching from Maine to Florida.

All the way down the Pacific Coast of the American continent good surfs can be found. In Mexico where the cost of a board confines the sport to the sons and daughters of the richer classes, there are miles of lonely beaches with good waves for the surfer on surfari. In Peru, the sport is well established, though the richer classes are the only ones who can afford the equipment and the cost of

A board rider's view of a big wave at Cronulla Point, N.S.W.

Trapped inside, a surfer about to go over the 'falls', while Ken Williams drops down the face of a big wave at Cronulla Point, N.S.W.

A tremendous 'throw-out' can be seen as this surfer fights to control his board while he accelerates down the wave.

Bobby Brown—at 12 years.

A wave that demands respect. A Sunset Beach boomer.

membership of the surfing clubs, the Waikiki and the Kon Tiki, near Lima. The surf in Peru is amazingly constant, at a size of from three to six feet, giving long rides. On the Atlantic coast the surf at Rio de Janeiro is even better and just as consistent as that of Peru, attracting riders from all over the world. Australia has an abundance of beaches with surfing conditions of all kinds, all around the 12,000 miles of coastline on beaches with such names as Dee Why, Bilgola, Fairy Bower, Voodoo Bay, Currumbin, Yellingup, Maroochydore, Noosa and many more with surfing conditions constant throughout the year, particularly in the sub-tropic north, along the Queensland coast. Despite the winning of two world championships out of the first four contested, surfing in Australia is still at the 'enormous potential' stage and when developed the country could become the world's surfing capital.

Bobby Brown showing the stylish control that won him blue ribbons.

Spectacular free-fall from George Grenough.

At dozens of spots in New Zealand, along the South African coastline between Capetown and Durban, in Morocco on the Atlantic swells, on the primitive, lonely beaches of Spain and Portugal, along the southwest coast of France, on the Jersey Island, the Canary Islands in mid-Atlantic, in Puerto Rico and Curacao, around the southern coast of England, in India and Ceylon, Israel and Japan, Ireland and Ecuador, wherever the sea makes waves on a country's shoreline, there are surfers, recreating in their own way, their individual Sport of Kings.

With the advent of the boards into surfing, the sport quickly developed its own language, with variations or 'dialects' differing in the different areas of the world where the waves break.

David Treloar at Angourie, N.S.W.

Locked in—a surfer trims hard to make the wave at Sandon Point, N.S.W.

A general guide is:

all-time: great, fantastic.

angle: riding across the face of a wave or toward the shoulder.

arch: a back bend used mainly in turns.

backing out: pulling off a wave.

back pedal: overlapping the feet in walking to the back of the board.

backwash: a wave washing back to seaward from the shore.

baggies: the large flap-legged boxer type shorts worn by the surfer.

bail out: to leave the board suddenly in the face of a wipe-out.

barge: a very heavy, large board.

beach break: waves breaking close inshore on sand.

big gun: a big-wave board, used mainly in the giant Hawaiian surfs and still at times in Australia.

blown out: a surf so whipped up by winds as to become unrideable.

bombed out: to be wiped out, or thrown off the board in a wave.

boomer, dumper: with blaster, whomper, crusher, terms to describe violent, hard breaking waves.

bottom turn: a turn on the front of a wave at the bottom of the wall.

carving up the mob: derived in Australia, to describe reckless riding through a crowd of body surfers or swimmers.

caught inside: a surfer shoreward of a breaking wave is considered to be caught inside.

channel: a deep spot where waves don't break and where the incoming waves retreat back to sea. Used for getting out.

chip: name given to first all-balsa wood boards constructed in the late forties. Much smaller than the giant planks, they were referred to as 'potato chips'. Also known as Malibu boards.

choppy: many little waves created by local winds, making a very bumpy and difficult surface to surf on.

classic: perfect surfing form; a perfect or fantastic day.

clean-up: a wave that breaks outside of most surfers, causing them to lose their boards, 'cleaning-up the area'.

climbing: steering the board up the face of the wave toward the top or crest.

close-out: when waves break all the way across a bay or normally safe channel, rendering a surf spot unrideable. When a spot is closed-out, it is usually considered too big to ride.

concave: a type of surfboard designed by Bob Simmons.

conservative: a rider who stays away from the curl or the hot part of the wave, taking no chances.

cornering: an Australian term for angling.

crack: Australian term for a ride. 'Crack a good wave.'

crest: the highest point of a wave before it breaks.

critical: a very steep and difficult-to-ride wave.

crouch: a leaning-forward, squatting position to
(1)   duck the breaking part of the wave,
(2)   reduce wind resistance, and
(3)   obtain better balance in the big-wave drop.

curl: the breaking part of the wave, spilling over and creating a space between the main body of the wave and the spilling crest.

custom surfboard: a surfboard built especially for the rider. His size, weight, and the type of riding he wishes to do are generally taken into consideration.

cut back: to turn back toward the curl or breaking part of the wave.

cut out: same as pull-out or kick-out. A second meaning is that of being forced out of the wave by another surfer, i.e., 'He cut me out.'

deck: the top surface of a surfboard.

dig a rail: when the side of the board or rail digs into the wave, usually ending in a wipe-out. Generally caused by poor positioning on a turn, trying to turn from too far forward.

ding: a hole in the surfboard.

double-ender: a surfboard that is almost symmetrical with a slightly pointed tip at both ends.

down: referring to the surf, the surf is flat or down.

down the mine: an Australian term for a wipe-out.

driving: exerting extra effort to trim the board and gain the most possible speed.

drop: the initial downward slide after taking off in a wave.

drop-in: sliding down the face of the wave immediately after it is caught.

dropping: moving down on the face of the wave toward the trough.

dump: a wipe-out in surfing. Often referred to in body surfing.

el spontanio: a squatting position where the surfer looks back between his legs. In a pure el spontanio the fingers must be interlocked behind the surfer's back.

elephant gun: same as big gun; a surfboard designed especially for the big surf or heavies.

face: the unbroken front of a wave between the crest and the trough.

fade: riding toward the curl or hot part of the wave before turning and riding across the face away from the curl. A manoeuvre used to stay in the hottest part of the wave.

fin: see skeg.

fins: rubber flippers used as aids in swimming or body surfing; called swim fins.

floater: a large, buoyant board.

foot paddle: while standing, dipping one foot over the side of the board and paddling to increase forward motion.

free fall: occasionally, while riding high or taking off on a very steep wave, a surfboard will slip out and the board and rider will fall in mid-air down the face of the wave. This is a free fall.

full suit: a rubber suit consisting of long pants, full jacket, long sleeves, hood, boots, and possibly gloves.

fun surf: small or medium surf not big enough to make the surfer think twice before taking off or to make him worry about taking a wipe-out.

glass-off: when the wind dies (usually in the afternoon), causing the water to become very smooth or glassy slick.

glassy: an extremely smooth surface or wave, usually giving off a glasslike reflection.

goofy-foot: a rider who surfs with his right foot as the lead foot.

grab the rail: when the surfer is about to be hit by the wave or white water, he grabs the rail of his board away from the wave, leans toward the wave, and pulls his board into the wave to keep from being knocked off and to continue on in the curl or on the unbroken wave ahead.

green: an unbroken wave; sometimes referring to the shoulder of a wave.

hanging five: five toes over the nose of the board.

hanging ten: ten toes over the nose of the board.

head dip: while riding, the surfer bends over, trying to stick his head into the wave or white water. If his head gets wet from the wave, this is a successful head dip.

314

heavies: the big surf.

highway surfer: one who spends all his time in the car and never gets to the surf.

ho-dad, ho-daddy: a greaser or hood from the back streets, generally with hopped-up car. May or may not be a surfer.

hollow: an extremely concave or curling wave.

hook: the curling part of the wave.

hot-dog: to perform or show a great deal of ability in the surf; usually denoted by fancy turns, walking the nose, and taking chances.

Huey: the Australian 'god' of the surf.

humpers: medium-to-large unbroken waves.

inshore: referring to either the beach or the area of water just off the beach.

inside: (a) shoreward of the normal breaking point of the waves; (b) completely within the curling part of the wave or inside the tunnel.

Kahuna: Hawaiian witch doctor adopted by modern surfers as an imaginary surfing god, as the Australian 'Huey'.

Kamaaina: an old-timer to the waves of Hawaii. In surfing—experienced.

kami-kaze: a planned wipe-out; taken on purpose with no hope of saving the board or avoiding the swim.

kelp skeg: a shallow or slowly tapered fin designed so as not to hang-up or catch on the kelp (seaweed).

kick-out: flipping the board over the back or through the back of a wave, while falling off the tail of the board into the wave. A kick-out is a last ditch effort to keep from losing your board.

knee paddling: paddling while balanced on the board in a kneeling position.

Kona wind: a south wind in the Hawaiian Islands, generally onshore at most of the southern exposure beaches. Occasionally offshore or glassy on the north shore.

kook: a beginner; know-nothing; generally blundering and in the way.

kook box: a paddle board.

lava tube: a hollow cave or tube carved out of the lava rock, generally referring to submarine caves beneath surfing spots.

left slide: a ride where the surfer slides to his left.

let down: a wave breaking.

line: a long wave.

line-up: the point where the waves are consistently starting to break.

lip: the fringing crest of the wave starting to break, but not yet curling.

locked in: surfer in a position where it is impossible to pull-out. Yet, the wave may still be makeable. He is considered locked in the curl.

log: a very heavy surfboard.

loomer: a big wave suddenly appearing outside.

looper: a wave that curls or throws out in front of itself, often breaking over a surfer so as to make his ride 'in the tunnel'.

Makaha board: a board designed in the 1950s, especially for riding through the Makaha bowl. The tail was pointed with a flat bottom and this design was supposed to help the board glide across the flat part of the wave and thus enable the surfer to make it through the 'bowl'. The board featured the sharp break-away edge on the bottom of the tail block.

Malibu board: the balsa wood board or 'chip' designed in the late forties and ridden predominantly at Malibu.

malihini: a newcomer to the Hawaiian Islands. Newcomers to the sport of surfing are also referred to as malihinis.

mat: a rubber mattress inflated and used to ride the waves. Some of the newer mats are constructed of plastic foam.

mat surfer: a surfer who rides waves with a rubber surf mat.

mob: an Australian term for a group of surfers —usually many.

mushy: a slow, sloppy wave that has little power.

mysterioso: an adornment' or surf trick,

popular in the late fifties. Created by Mickey Muñoz, the stance is with the surfer bending over, hiding his head in his hands.

outrigger: a pontoon used to stabilize a narrow, dug-out-type canoe.

outrigger canoe: a canoe employing the use of an outrigger.

outside: (a) referring to any point seaward of the normal breaking point of the wave; (b) an exclamation used to describe an approaching set of waves.

out-the-back: an Australian term for outside or seaward.

over the falls: the pouring part of the breaking wave is considered the falls. A surfer caught and carried over in the breaking part goes 'over the falls'.

paddleboard: a square-sided, hollow surfcraft usually constructed of plywood.

paipo board: a small bellyboard used in the Hawaiian Islands.

paraffin: a wax most commonly applied on the deck of a surfboard to reduce slickness.

peak: a narrow, humping wave that has little wall, generally tapering fast from the middle or high point of the wave to almost flat on the shoulders; the highest point of the wave.

pearl or pearling: while riding, the nose of the surfboard goes beneath the surface and continues downward, usually throwing the rider off (originally taken from pearl diving).

peeler: a fast, curling wave that curls perfectly without sectioning ahead.

performer: a hot-dogger who does a lot of turning and creative riding on a wave.

pig board: a surfboard with an extremely pointed nose, with the widest area of the board toward the rear.

pintail: a surfboard with a long, drawn-out, pointed tail.

plank: name given to heavy boards, usually referring to the redwood giants ridden prior to the 1950s.

pole set: waves breaking adjacent to or immediately inside of a large pole jutting out of the water at Ala Moana in Hawaii. Generally takes surf of at least eight feet or larger to break by or outside the pole.

poly: Australian term used for foam surfboard.

polystyrene foam: a type of foam which differs from polyurethane foam only in that a different type of gluing agent is used. Owing to problems with glassing, this foam is seldom used in surfboard construction.

polyurethane foam: a type of plastic foam that is presently most used in the construction of surfboards.

pop-out: a mass-produced surfboard; little hand work involved.

pounder: an unusually hard-breaking wave.

pour over: when a wave breaks, it is pouring over. An over-the-falls wipe-out may also be considered a pour over.

psyched out: mentally incapacitated; generally referring to a surfer's reaction to the big surf. To become frightened, shook up, or psyched out.

pull-out: steering the board over or through the back of the wave, as to end the ride.

push through: originally a method of getting your surfboard through the wave. The surfer climbed off his board and, holding on to the rear of the board, pushed it ahead of him through the wave. Push through has now come to mean any method of going through the surf or white water.

quasimodo: a hunchback position where one arm is stetched forward, the other arm stretched to the rear.

Queen Mary: a board too big for the rider, usually very large and buoyant.

rails: the rounded sides of the surfboard.

reef: a line or ridge of rock, coral, or sand lying at or near the surface of the water. Reefs are important in the forming of good surfing waves.

resin: the liquid plastic that is coated on the fibreglass to bind it to the surfboard.

reverse kick-out: same as kick-out, with the surfer executing a half spinner as he kicks his board out of the wave.

reverse take-off: a skeg-first take-off where the surfer lies on his board and once in the wave spins his board around and stands up, riding in the correct manner.

right of way: the surfer who is already on the wave and riding has the right of way and others coming into the wave should respect this right.

right slide: a ride where the surfer slides to his right.

rip tide: a current or river of water moving seaward, generally accompanying big surf where a lot of water is moving toward shore and must have a way to get back out to sea.

rocker: (a) an Australian ho-dad; a 'rock and roller'; (b) the curvature of a surfboard— from front to back.

roll: while paddling directly into an oncoming broken wave, the surfer turns his board over— bottom up—sometimes wrapping his legs around the board while the wave passes over. After the wave passes, he rolls the board over and continues paddling outside.

roller: a wave that does not curl or tube; the white water slides down the face of the wave.

roto-moto: continuous spinners.

rubber arms: a description for the surfer who doesn't paddle hard enough to get a wave because it's too large.

sand bar: a mound or plateau of sand caused by surf or sea currents and occasionally acting as an underwater reef, creating good surfing waves. Sand bars are not permanent.

scratching: paddling hard.

section: a part of the breaking wave.

sectioning: a wave that is not breaking evenly; breaking ahead of itself.

shelf: referring to a reef or rock formation underwater that drops off sharply. Shore-bound waves hitting this shelf often jump up, creating a larger and faster-breaking wave than if the wave ran its normal course. Waimea Bay is a good example of a shelf-type break.

shooting the curl: riding through the curling or tubing part of the wave; making a hot section.

shore pound: a very hard-breaking wave, usually thick and pounding right on the shore.

shorebreak: waves breaking very close to the beach.

shoulder: the unbroken, tapering part of the wave from the curl or white water.

shoulder turn: a turn where the shoulders are rotated in the direction of the turn.

shuffle: moving toward the nose of the board without crossing foot over foot, usually a sliding manoeuvre.

skeg: the fin or rudder of a board.

slide: to ride either left or right somewhat parallel to shore.

slope: the curvature of the face of an unbroken wave.

slot: the perfect spot in the wave; in the curl.

snuff out: a fast wipe-out where the surfer is covered by the curl or tube and either disappears or is blasted off his board.

soup or froth: same as white water or foam.

spin out: the skeg or rudder comes out of the water, usually on a turn or on a very fast or steep wave.

spinner or 360°: a surfer turning around on his board until he faces the same direction in which he started.

spitter: air caught in the tunnel or curl must go somewhere when the wave collapses. If there is an open end to the wave, the air and spray hiss out of this opening and the wave is then called a 'spitter'.

spoon: referring to the upturned nose of a surfboard; also called scoop. The spooned or scooped nose was designed to keep the surfboard from pearling.

squaretail: a surfboard with the tail squared off rather than rounded or pointed.

stacked up: (a) several surfers grouped closely —one above another—in a wave; (b) a group of many lines or waves coming toward shore.

stall: a slowing of the board while waiting for the wave to steepen ahead.

standing island: a type of pull-out where the rider slashes through the back of a wave, standing toward the front or on the nose of his board.

stick: a surfboard.

stoked: excited or jazzed, usually about the surf.

storm surf: waves tossed up or generated by a local storm, generally not clean surf and usually big.

straight off: a ride straight toward shore without turning or angling, directly in line with the movement of the wave.

straighten off: a turning from a definite angle across the wave to directly toward shore or in the same direction as the wave is actually moving.

stringers: strips of wood laminated into a surfboard, generally used for strength or design.

stripes: decorations applied on the outside of a surfboard.

strips: narrow pieces of wood used to reinforce a surfboard; sometimes used for decoration only.

submarine: a board too small for the rider, floating him under the surface.

suck out: a wave that breaks extremely fast, throwing out in front of itself, creating a space, tube, or tunnel. Caused by the wave coming suddenly over a shallow spot and throwing forward.

Surf Day: a day in Peru when the surf is too large for freighters to dock at piers and load or discharge their cargoes.

surf safari: a trip in search of surf, generally considered to be more than just a short drive.

surfing knobs, bumps, knots, etc.: calcium deposits over the knees and on the feet where the knees and feet come into contact with the board while kneeling. Medically termed Osgood-Schlatter disease, it is also known as housemaid's knee. Can be very painful when just starting to surf or just returning from a long lay-off. Particularly common among young surfers.

swell: either one unbroken wave or all of the waves coming from one particular storm. Example: a storm in the North Pacific sends waves to the north shore of Hawaii that are ten feet the first day, twenty feet the second day, and twelve feet the third day, all with good shape. The surfers would refer to this surf as a good swell.

switchfoot: a surfer who rides with either right foot or left foot forward, depending on which direction he is headed—usually trying to face the wave at all times.

tail: the rear of the board to which the skeg is attached.

tail flutter: on bigger waves the tail of the board may sometimes go out of control and become very unstable. This is caused by too wide a tail, a board bottom that is too flat, or by riding too far to the rear of the board.

take-off: to launch into a wave; to begin a ride.

take-off point: the exact spot where the waves are consistently breaking in such a way as to provide a good ride for the surfer.

taking gas: getting a wipe-out; being knocked off the board.

tandem: two persons riding one surfboard, generally a boy and a girl.

toes over: any number of toes over the nose of your surfboard; also referred as hanging five or hanging ten.

top-to-bottom: a wave that pours out in front when it breaks, with the initial point of contact matching the height of the wave.

trade wind: a wind that blows toward the equator from the northeast on the north side of the equator and from the southeast on the south side; the prevailing winds in the Hawaiian Islands. The trade winds generally blow off-shore at most of the good Hawaiian surfing beaches.

trail foot: the foot toward the tail of the board in a normal stance.

trimming: steering the board into a position nearest to parallel with the line of the wave, thus gaining the most possible speed out of the wave.

tube: the space formed by a particularly long or fast wave throwing out in front of itself.

undertow: a current of water moving beneath and in a different direction from the surface water; said especially of a seaward current beneath breaking surf.

up: referring to the surf; the surf is up or big.

wahine: a girl.

walk the nose: foot over foot walking toward the nose of the board.

wall: the face of a wave before it has broken.

wax: paraffin wax used to coat the glassy surface of a surfboard to reduce the slickness.

wet suit: a neoprene rubber suit designed to hold water within the foam. The water soon reaches body temperature, thus keeping the surfer warm.

white cap: a wind-blown chop or wave with its crest broken into white foam; generally rolls a short distance and backs off.

white water: soup or foam; the result of a breaking wave.

wind lift: offshore winds blowing up the face of the wave, making it very difficult to drop in and sometimes blowing the surfer and his board back over the top.

wind peaks: waves with a short wave length caused by strong, local winds; very narrow and generally choppy.

BIBLIOGRAPHIC NOTE

Material on surfing's origin and early history is drawn from *Surfing, The Sport of Hawaiian Kings* by Ben. R. Finney and J. D. Houston (Charles E. Tuttle Co., Rutland, Vermont and Tokyo, 1965) and from the following series of articles by Ben. R. Finney:

'Surfboarding in Oceania: its Pre-European Distribution', *Wiener Voelkerkundliche Mitteilungen*, II, 23-36, Vienna, 1959
'Surfboarding in West Africa', *Wiener Voelkerkundliche Mitteilungen*, V, 41-42, Vienna, 1962

'Surfing in Ancient Hawaii', *Journal of the Polynesian Society*, LXVIII, 327-347, Wellington, 1959.
'The Development and Diffusion of Modern Hawaiian Surfing', *Journal of the Polynesian Society*, LXIX, 315-331, Wellington, 1962

Readers interested in a more comprehensive analysis of surfing's history, or in referring to the extensive but scattered documentary sources on the sport, should consult these works.

INDEX

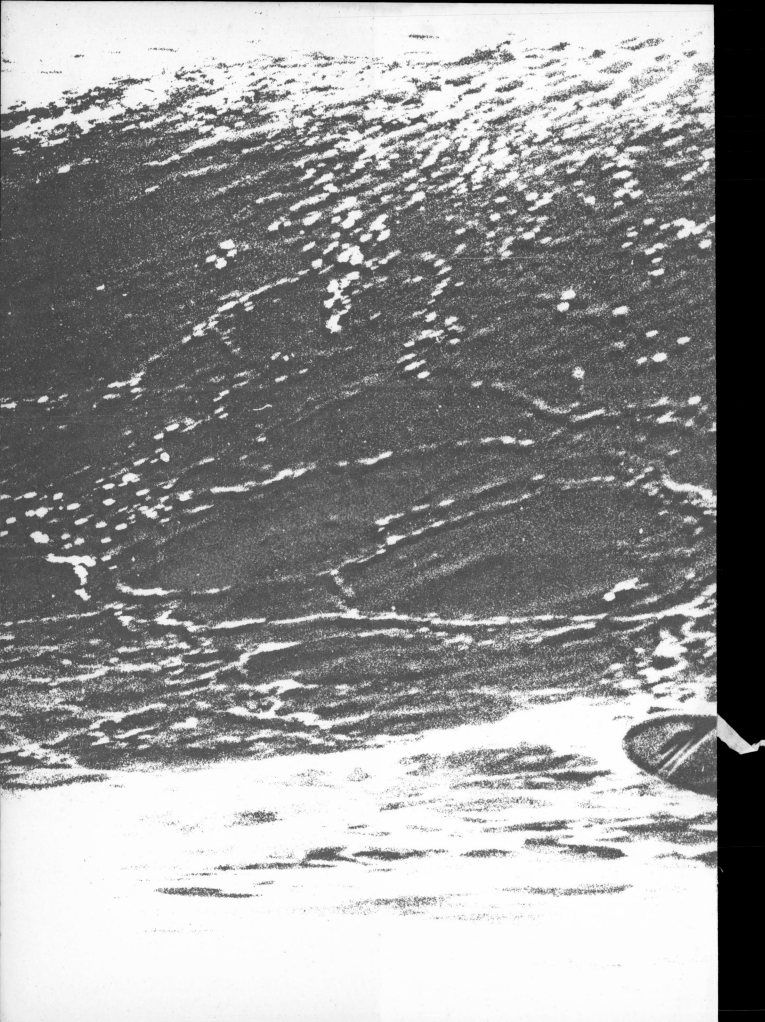